Scam Survivor is a must read f̶̶̶̶̶̶̶̶̶̶̶̶̶̶̶̶̶̶̶̶̶̶̶̶ you've
fallen victim to f̶̶̶̶̶̶̶̶̶̶̶̶̶̶̶̶̶̶̶̶̶̶̶̶̶̶̶̶̶̶̶̶̶̶̶̶̶̶ ith the
story of his devas̶̶̶̶̶̶̶̶̶̶̶̶̶̶̶̶̶̶̶̶̶̶̶̶̶̶̶̶̶̶̶̶̶̶ ier and
how he and his wi̶̶̶̶̶̶̶̶̶̶̶̶̶̶̶̶̶̶̶̶̶̶̶̶̶̶̶̶̶̶̶̶̶̶̶̶ This is
both a cautionary̶̶̶̶̶̶̶̶̶̶̶̶̶̶̶̶̶̶̶̶̶̶̶̶̶̶̶̶̶̶̶̶̶̶̶̶̶̶ actical
help. It will enligh̶̶̶̶̶̶̶̶̶̶̶̶̶̶̶̶̶̶̶̶̶̶̶̶̶̶̶̶̶̶̶̶̶̶̶̶

Dr Jo̶̶ ?overty
̶̶ eader"
D.1̶̶ ...... of the University of Bradford

Jonathan has objectively, yet personally, drawn us into a nine-month period of his life which profoundly changed his life.

His inner resilience, faith and strength, together with wonderful people and helpful outside resources helped him to overcome adversity. He takes us on his campaign, showing considerable practical wisdom as he succeeds in retrieving money that he lost through a scam. His personal emotional journey through this traumatic experience will, I believe, be helpful to others who confront similar situations.

Scam Survivor should be read by the most tech-savvy folk around! The rest of us should also take the time to acquaint ourselves with the sophisticated, rapidly evolving and grubby world of cyber-crime to protect ourselves and our finances.

Stephen Critchlow, MRCPsych.,
Consultant Psychiatrist

Scam Survivor is both an excellent resource and timely warning to us all that predators are watching and looking for opportunities to get our money. This is an honest account from Jonathan Leakey that we can never afford to let down our guard and assume we will never be the victim of a scam. I have over 34 years policing experience and firmly believe that one of the best policing tools available to us all is prevention. "Prevention is better than cure". Reading Scam Survivor might save you or your family significant financial loss, emotional trauma and embarrassment. We cannot afford to ignore that we live in a world where evil and unscrupulous individuals and highly sophisticated crime gangs are looking for opportunities to steal from the vulnerable or from those who are ignorant of the risks they pose to us all. I recommend you read this book as a warning and way to ensure you are on your guard against the global growing threat from fraudsters and thieves wanting to steal your money.

Chief Superintendent Stephen Cargin,
(former) Head of Justice Police Service Northern Ireland

SCAM SURVIVOR

HOW ONE VICTIM FOUGHT BACK

Jonathan Leakey

Scam Survivor

© Copyright 2020 by Jonathan Leakey

All rights reserved. No part of this publication may be reproduced, distributed or transmitted in any form or by any means, including photocopying, recording, or other electronic or mechanical methods, without the prior written permission of the publisher, except in the case of brief quotations embodied in critical reviews and certain other non-commercial uses permitted by copyright law.

Although the author and publisher have made every effort to ensure that the information in this book was correct at press time, the author and publisher do not assume and hereby disclaim any liability to any party for any loss, damage, or disruption caused by errors or omissions, whether such errors or omissions result from negligence, accident, or any other cause.

Adherence to all applicable laws and regulations, including international, federal, state and local governing professional licensing, business practices, advertising, and all other aspects of doing business in the US, Canada or any other jurisdiction is the sole responsibility of the reader and consumer.

Neither the author nor the publisher assumes any responsibility or liability whatsoever on behalf of the consumer or reader of this material. Any perceived slight of any individual or organisation is purely unintentional.

The resources in this book are provided for informational purposes only and should not be used to replace the advice of relevant professionals.

Neither the author nor the publisher can be held responsible for the use of the information provided within this book. Please always consult your bank before making any decision regarding your own account(s) and the fraud protection they recommend for those with accounts held with them, both online and otherwise. Please always consult a trained professional before making any decision regarding anti-virus software for your PC, laptop, mobile or other device.

This book is a work of non-fiction.

Author: Jonathan Leakey

Editor: Joel Leakey

Cover designed by Jennifer Harte

Formatter: InkSmith Editorial Services

First Edition: September 2020

ISBN: 978-1-8381289-0-6 (paperback)

ISBN: 978-1-8381289-1-3 (e-book)

Contents

Preface VII
Introduction 1

Part 1: Our Story — 5

Smished! 7
The Warning Signs 21
Hindsight Is a Wonderful Thing! 27
Fighting Back, and Our Last Resort 35
The Nightmare Ends 47
Healing From The Trauma 53

Part 2: How To Fight Back — 61

Draw Up a Plan of Action; Work Your Plan 63
Keep a Record 69
Identify Your Allies and Build a Support Team 71
Determine the Parameters of Your Case 73
Be Clear: Were You "Grossly Negligent"? 77
Communicate Well with Your Bank 81
Aim High! 89

Part 3: Know Your Enemy Know Your Allies — 97

Appendices — 109

Statutory and Other Bodies Dealing with Fraud Cases (UK) 111
Statutory and Other Bodies Dealing with Fraud Cases (USA) 119
Statutory and Other Bodies Dealing with Fraud Cases (EU) 123
Media Coverage of Fraud Cases 125
Published Research on Fraud (UK) 127
Acknowledgements 129

This book is dedicated to my wife, Tricia, who stood by me through the trauma of our experience with fraud, never once pointing the finger, and always believing we would get through this. You were, and are, my tower of strength.

You are now 20 times more likely to be robbed while at your computer ... than held up in the street ...

—*Daily Telegraph, Martin Evans, crime correspondent 21 July 2016*

PREFACE

Don't put off reading this book. Fraudsters are constantly dreaming up new and more cunning ways of deceiving us. Even tech-savvy millennials and fraud experts have been hooked.

This book will help you to spot a potential scam and avoid being conned. It will also help readers who have been deceived by a scam and lost money to face the trauma, manage their emotions, and come out winners the other side.

Part One is our story, interspersed with the lessons we learned along the way. **Part Two** and **Part Three** are "How To" sections on how we campaigned to recover our money. It is also where to find expert help and advice either if you've fallen victim to a scam or are looking to protect yourself better. If you are wanting a straightforward "How To" then you may choose to skip straight to the **Part Two** and **Part Three**. However, we would recommend starting from the beginning as the moment by moment account of our experience narrated in **Part One**, combined with the lessons learned, will also inform and raise awareness. Finally, the **Appendices** list a wide range of organisations and resources dedicated to helping the victims of fraud and those looking to be more vigilant.

This account of our experience of a serious fraud scam in March 2018 cost us £25,000 in a matter of minutes. It has been written for two types of reader. First, it is for those who have fallen victim to online banking fraud and are interested to see how another victim reacted to the experience and, ultimately, found resolution. Secondly, it is aimed at those who may not have been a victim of fraud, but who are keen to know of the danger signs in order to protect themselves.

We make no claim to being experts in the field of fraud and readers should consult the various resources available online and in bookstores. These include their bank's own guidance and also that of the Consumer Association *Which?* In addition, the Financial Conduct Authority's and the Financial Ombudsman Service's websites are helpful. A list of the various resources and web addresses is given in the **Appendices** at the end of this book. We are able, however, to testify of our first-hand experience and the impact it had on our lives. It will help the reader to be more alert to the potential threats that could come at any moment down any one of the connected technologies we have at our finger tips.

Online fraud and cyber-crime, in general, are fast-evolving and multi-faceted threats. In 2018-19 in the UK there were a number of "Brexit scams" doing the rounds, exploiting the confusion and uncertainty surrounding the UK's departure from the EU.[1] 2020 was the year of COVID-19, and sure enough the scammers were exploiting that crisis to steal from unsuspecting individuals.[2]

The reader will gain understanding from this book as to how some scams work. We trust, thereby, that

---
1 For information on Brexit scams see: https://www.which.co.uk/consumer-rights/advice/brexit-scams (accessed 22/5/2019).
2 For information on COVID-19 scams see: https://www.which.co.uk/news/2020/04/coronavirus-scams-how-to-spot-them-and-stop-them/ (accessed 19/5/2020).

he/she will come away better able to spot a scam and be protected from being conned. For those who fall victim we want to give encouragement not to give up the fight to recover your losses, and guidance as to where you can look for help.

Scam Survivor tells the story of one couple's strategy for recovering money lost through fraud, and also highlights some keys for recovery from the trauma that many victims of scams experience. It is not a substitute for the advice some readers may need to obtain from professional financial advisors, or medical or psychological experts in the field of trauma recovery. It is not wise to assume that what works for one individual will necessarily work for another.

INTRODUCTION

Fraud is the fastest growing crime in the world. Fraud attacks and scams are the most frequently carried out crimes. The UK's Consumers' Association *Which?* says "fraud is now at record levels, with more than five million scams costing Britons a mind-boggling £9bn each year".[3] The Crime Survey for England and Wales 2015 showed that you are now 20 times more likely to be robbed while at your computer by a criminal based overseas than held up in the street.[4] The report listed phishing, identity theft, hacking and online harassment as four of the commonest examples of cyber-crime. Being mugged on the street can be highly traumatic, but getting "cyber-mugged" can be equally distressing, if not more so. The victim of a cyber-crime will probably get away without any physical harm being inflicted on him or her. However, the experience often involves them losing much more than the contents of their bank account. It will invariably leave emotional and psychological scars that can take years to heal.

---

3 Consumers' Association Which? article on fraud levels: https://campaigns.which.co.uk/scams-fraud-safeguard/ (accessed 25/3/2019).
4 Daily Telegraph report on the findings of the Crime Survey for England and Wales (2015) https://www.telegraph.co.uk/news/2016/07/21/one-in-people-now-victims-of-cyber-crime/ (accessed 25/3/2019).

We make it too easy for them ...

Fraudsters are the primary people to blame, of course, but we make it too easy for them. Naivety and ignorance on the part of the average person of the methods used by fraudsters are widespread. A failure to take certain key steps to protect ourselves, our hard earned money, and property certainly makes it easier for these criminals to succeed. Furthermore, many victims of fraud lack the knowledge of what to do once they've been targeted and may not readily have the courage, perseverance and circle of support to try and recover their losses.

Two types of reader...

For those readers who have fallen victim to fraud we hope this book encourages you not to lie down and assume your money is lost forever. You are not alone, and nor were you necessarily grossly negligent, whatever your bank may tell you. We hope that, reading this will motivate you to pick yourself up off the ground and begin to fight your corner, find who your allies are and get the help you need.

For those who have not yet fallen victim to fraud, we hope from the bottom of our hearts that you won't have to go through an experience like ours. To that end we say "forewarned is forearmed", and we trust that our story gives you an insight into what you can do to protect yourself from the fraudster, and to spot a scam when it comes calling.

Although I live in the United Kingdom, this book has world-wide relevance. Even though I was at home when I was targeted, our attackers may well have been operating from outside the UK. Cyber-criminals respect no geographical boundaries, and their deceptions are repeated the world over, often in slightly different guises.

Nowadays, we need to be vigilant every time we go online, whether to shop, use email, message or visit our favourite social networking sites. We also need to be vigilant when out and about as the means to steal our bank data or identity can be hidden in a small portable gadget that covertly swipes your data as you brush past it. Equally it might be attached unobtrusively to an ATM (cash machine).

While it took us nine months and a lot of hard work to turn our situation around, the decision from day one to fight our case gave us something positive to focus on and throw our energies into. It also helped us beat the self-destructive blame-game, bitterness and depression in which we could so easily have wallowed. My wife and I came out of it as stronger people, with a new community of friends and with the wisdom, experience and empathy to help others going through traumatic experiences.

Part 1
OUR STORY

1

SMISHED!

A form of phishing, smishing is when someone tries to trick you into giving them your private information via a text or SMS message.[5]

One of the stereotypical cyber-crime scenarios is an elderly person falling victim to an obvious email scam. But that's not who most criminals target.
— *IT Manager Daily*

Fraud can happen to anybody.

It has happened to people who might think they were fraud-proof. Senior police officers and even fraud specialists have fallen victim!

If you are young and tech-savvy, it is important not to think that you are therefore immune to being deceived by cyber-criminals.

The rest of the quote above from the *IT Manager Daily* makes it clear that it's actually younger people, those who spend most of their time online, that are more at risk:

> "... It's the tech-savvy folks who are the most likely victims of cyber-crime, according to a recent study by security

---
[5] NortonLifeLock Inc https://us.norton.com/internetsecurity-emerging-threats-what-is-smishing.html (Accessed 20/07/2020).

vendor Symantec. The group that gets in the most trouble online: men aged 18-31 who access the Internet from mobile devices. According to Symantec, 80% of those people have fallen prey to cyber-crime at least once in their lives. The reason: They spend the most time online, so they[6] give criminals the most opportunities to attack."

In fact a 2018 report by the US Federal Trade Commission found that

"Consumers in their twenties reported losing money to fraud more often than those over age 70. For example, among people aged 20-29 who reported fraud, 40 percent indicated they lost money. In comparison, just 18 percent of those 70 and older who reported fraud indicated they lost any money. However, when these older adults did report losing money to a scammer, the median amount lost was greater". [7]

While I do not fall into the 18-31 age bracket (I was 56 when I fell victim), I do have a PhD in computer-assisted language learning, and I spend a significant amount of time online or working on computers. I am also the Neighbourhood Watch officer for my street and regularly receive and pass on to my neighbours, many of them elderly, warnings and advice as to the dangers of cyber-crime (and other types of criminality) and how they might best avoid falling victim.

My wife and I are naturally cautious and risk-averse by personality, and this includes how we spend

---

[6] IT Manager Daily article http://www.itmanagerdaily.com/most-likely-cyber-crime-victim/ September 14, 2011. (Accessed 12/06/2019).
[7] FTC Releases Annual Summary of Complaints Reported by Consumers https://www.ftc.gov/news-events/press-releases/2018/03/ftc-releases-annual-summary-complaints-reported-consumers (Accessed 22/10/2019).

our money. We also have always taken care to follow advice on staying up-to-date with the anti-virus protection on our computers. We are careful at ATM machines and regularly check our bank statements against expenses. I thought I was quite scam-proof!

Through the smallest of cracks

Our brush with a fraudster came out of the blue. The scammers' deception allowed them to slip through the smallest of cracks in our defences.

You may ask, "Why is someone, who was themselves scammed, qualified to help me avoid being scammed?" The fact that a professional person like me could fall victim to fraud should serve as a sobering warning to anyone who might be lulled into complacency, thinking that it could never happen to them.

We also now know what it's like to go through the trauma of a fraud experience and are, therefore, well qualified to share our insights as to how a fraud unfolds. We have discovered what not to do, and what actions need to be taken to get back on one's feet, and stand a reasonable chance of recovering one's money.

We had to learn quickly and intentionally to protect our emotional and mental health. Furthermore, as we journeyed the aftermath and set about recovering our losses, we carried out a significant amount of research into modern-day scams, much of which we have made available in this book.

Here is our story...

The date is Tuesday 13th March 2018.

I am nearly finished with what I am hoping might possibly be my last ever pile of marking and I am looking forward to relaxing with my mid-morning cup of coffee. As I work through the pile of student scripts my laptop is in front of me; my iPhone sits to the right of my laptop. Various messages have been coming in from time to time, on mute. I know they are there, and have no intention of touching any of them until I have finished the marking.

11:33am – I now pick up my phone to check my messages. I scan the last text which is from my bank, and immediately my stress levels go up a notch or two as I read the words: "xxxx BANK has noticed your debit card was recently used on 13-3-2018 11:28:03, at AMAZON ONLINE STORE for 2499.00 GBP." I read it a couple of times to try to understand what it is about. Figure 1 below gives the full wording of this text. We have chosen not to mention our bank's name in this book. We have substituted for its name the capitalised words "OURBANK".

In previous years I might have laughed and happily ignored the message, as our bank balance in that particular account had never amounted to such dizzy heights as a couple of grand! There are two reasons why I am worried this time.

> **OURBANK** has noticed your debit card was recently used on 13-03-2018 11:28:03, at AMAZON ONLINE STORE for 2499.00 GBP. If not you please urgently call fraud prevention on **0330**....... Or Intl **+44330**...... Do not reply by **SMS**

Figure 1: the first message from the fraudster – the fake fraud at 11:33am Tuesday 13th March

The first is because I know we have a good deal more than the £2,499 in our current account as my wife has recently taken early retirement and received a package from her work-place. I have also recently taken a severance package from my university who were imposing swingeing cuts on its staffing levels.

Secondly, I am utterly convinced, OURBANK has contacted me. I have good reason to believe so.

18 months previously, we had benefited from an authentic warning from OURBANK on this text service. At that time, a scammer had attempted to authorise a purchase via our Facebook account and the transfer had been blocked. I have good reason to trust this source.

Also I trust my phone. As far as I know my brand of phone is secure. I also thought I knew about phishing scams and knew these were primarily email scams, usually from overseas and easily-spotted crude deceptions.

Smishing = ???

Neither my wife nor I knew anything of a variant of phishing known as *smishing*, and I certainly didn't suspect that anyone could infiltrate a fraudulent message into my bank's own text-stream. My bank certainly hasn't informed us about these types of attack. The trap is laid and I am about to fall into it.

The message says: "If not you please urgently call fraud prevention on 0330…" I am now, of course, very eager to stop what I believe is an Amazon purchase using my debit card. For all I know it is happening here and now. What is there to stop them from making further purchases if this one goes through? So I go ahead and click on the 0330 link.

That is when the real fraud begins!

Unlike many cold-calls that we get that are obviously from call-centres outside the UK, this person introduces herself as "Tanya" and speaks my language fluently, with a calm and reassuring voice. She has me convinced I am dealing with my bank.

I explain why I am calling. She then asks me to hang up and dial again which I do. She then proceeds in a smooth and convincing manner to persuade me of the immediate danger to my account and the need to block the card straightaway and, if possible, get the purchase halted. As she is talking, I am at the same time scrolling back on my phone to check this really is someone from the bank talking to me. What convinces me is viewing recent confirmatory texts from the bank linked to various previous genuine online purchases I had made and knew about. Fear makes me want her to go ahead and resolve this threat. She exploits that fear, and convinces me that I have to act quickly.

Nothing out of the ordinary?

She tells me she needs to run through some security questions to confirm my identity: name, first line of address, and date of birth. There is nothing out of the ordinary. Then she asks the questions that, looking back with the benefit of hindsight, I now know were the fraudulent questions the bank would never have asked. These include my online security number and 4-digit passcode, followed by the unique single-use 4-digit number we have to read off from the key-card OURBANK provides us with whenever we sign up to online banking.

All the while I am responding, with adrenaline pumping, believing I have to act swiftly to salvage the £2,499 that I have been made to believe is at risk. "Tanya" then takes me through this process and twice asks for the 4-digit passcode. She causes me to believe this is all about checking the money is still in my account and that my debit card is blocked. I thank her for her help and the conversation ends.

As soon as the phone call ends, I go online to see if anything is happening on my account. Have I indeed lost that £2,499 to the supposed debit card fraud? Has the bank official caught it in time? I go through my usual routine of inserting customer online number, then security number then the key number. Then ... nothing! I just can't get into my account. I repeat the process. Still no access. Once more, again to no avail. What is going on? A slight panic is beginning to stir in me.

Cyber-mugged!

Now I notice the fraud warning on the bank's web page, to the effect that there are fraudsters currently active, and to make sure you do not divulge key security information. It is at this point that the enormity of what is, at that very moment, taking place hits me like a sledge-hammer.

How can I describe the swirling emotions that rise up and threaten to drown me at that very moment? Helplessness, despair, panic and horror crash over my head. Is this really happening? Can I undo this? Is it too late to fix? How much might they have taken? Is this for real?

How does one describe the experience of being traumatised? For me it is the horror of our private world and financial security being invaded, of having been mugged, robbed, and deceived by the person I have wrongly trusted. This is compounded by the accompanying feelings of stupidity, gullibility and self-reproach.

The time is now 12:10pm - I ring OURBANK's Fraud Team's emergency helpline and they are able to confirm that £25,000 has just been transferred out of our account. This is the maximum amount that could have been transferred in one 24-hour period - at least from a personal bank account such as ours. The employee on the other end of the line says she can do absolutely nothing to stop the transfer as it had already taken place, and in all likelihood our money has already been moved on further. She asks me to email to her screenshots of the texts I have received which I do. The straw we are both clutching at is the hope of being able to trace the money to the recipient account, whose sort code and account number are visible on my account. My hope is that my money is still in that recipient account, and thereby potentially recoverable.

Into a "mule" account

I only found out later from OURBANK's Fraud Team that, at this point, the money was being transferred by the fraudsters to a Barclays account in England. They had then arranged for it immediately to go out of this so-called "mule account" to multiple other accounts so as to make it almost impossible to trace. When I rang Barclays later, I was told that they couldn't deal with me on this as it was a bank-to-bank issue, and they would respond only to enquiries from OURBANK staff.[8]

The morning after the scam, Wednesday 14th March, I rang OURBANK's fraud emergency line to let the fraud department know who I was and to see if any progress had been made. I was told it was still the early stages of the enquiry so not to expect a call in the next few days. No-one from the Fraud Team of OURBANK told me to contact the police and we lost valuable time by wrongly assuming the bank was liaising with them. As it was, we only received this advice from the bank manager the following day. I found out weeks later when the bank confirmed the money was unrecoverable, that the fraud then became an official criminal investigation.

---

[8] Note that since September 2018 banks are now required to help customers check who they are paying. This new service called Confirmation of Payee (CoP) has been designed to help protect your payments from scams, fraudsters and payments going to the wrong account. While this may not prevent what happened to us, it will prevent people paying standing orders and CHAPS payments to the wrong account numbers, or to fraudulent accounts that don't match the legitimate account details.

At this stage we were completely unaware of what *smishing* was. We couldn't believe that OURBANK, or any bank for that matter, would allow a five-figure sum to be transferred so easily out of an account without robust checks from the bank.

The night before the scam, the bank had sent a vague warning down the same text-line that fraudsters were up to something. The message we received gave no indication of the nature of the fraud, the scam SMS message the fraudsters were using and what action to take if we received such a message.

What is more, I never received any further communication initiated by the Fraud Team; a reflection perhaps that they were overloaded having to deal with various fraud events. I was left wondering how many more serious fraud events like ours there could be that would keep them so busy and thus not be in a position to return our calls or follow up our case! Our experience at this time, with both banks involved, was a mixture of frustration and infuriation that it was so hard to contact them. When we finally did speak to them they either said they couldn't help us at this stage or promised return calls which often never transpired. Many days seemed to be wasted waiting on progress reports that never materialised.

Thursday 15th March 15:19 - "C.", the manager of my local branch called me to ask me to come in and see her (arranged for 10am the next day), and also advised me that, if I hadn't already done so, to inform the police.

Thursday 15th March 17:35 - I rang the local Police non-emergency number to inform them of the crime. They gave me a crime reference number, and later on that evening a constable came to visit and provided much needed reassurance. She informed us of Action Fraud and promised to set up our Action Fraud report, which then generated a National Crime Reference Number and Action Fraud reference number.

25,000 new cases every month!

It is definitely worth informing your local police force as soon as possible after the event. One obvious reason is to ensure that you are given a crime reference number and to join the Action Fraud database of live cases. It is also important to submit any developments as soon as they occur. Action Fraud are inundated with cases; most messages we received from them were automated messages which emphasised that they were receiving 25,000 new cases every month! This was not much help or encouragement to us! We never did receive anything of substance relating to our case from Action Fraud.

It is impossible to overstate the value of the emotional support provided by this particular constable. To have a friendly and sympathetic face from a statutory authority appearing at our door was so reassuring. We found out later that this same constable had taken our case to her heart. On her own initiative she had subsequently put in many extra hours chasing up our case. In fact, she made more progress than OURBANK's fraud team, which was just stunning and very uplifting for us. Even though her efforts ultimately did not lead to a prosecution or the recovery of our money from the fraudsters, to know that someone official out there had taken a personal interest in our case and had gone out of her way to try and get resolution for us was exceptional.

Friday 16th March 10:00am – still reeling from the blow of the fraud attack, we went in to our branch to meet with the manager and her colleague. We gave a summary of what had happened three days previously. Our bank manager confessed to being new to this crime of which we had been a victim. This kind of fraud was very new, she told us, though we found out later it had been known about by the banking world for at least ten years. Her colleague warned us that it was unlikely we would ever recover our loss or be reimbursed as we had divulged our pass-code and key numbers to the fraudster. We were offered a loan to tide us over!

On Friday 16th March - early evening our bank manager rang to inform us she had submitted our complaint to the bank's fraud team. There had been no progress in the investigation to report.

Saturday 17th March morning - I rang the fraud department to ask if our MasterCard account had also been raided. Thankfully it hadn't.[9]

A key encounter, and ally

Monday 19th March - I was still reeling from what had happened less than a week earlier. Part of our initial coping strategy was to keep doing the things that made up our normal routine. For me, this day meant taking my wife to her weekly portrait class. Sitting in the car outside I rang a friend who was a retired lawyer. He gave me some useful and wide-ranging advice, which helped form the backbone of a "campaign strategy" for fighting back.[10] It was so reassuring to receive helpful and trustworthy advice early on. A suggestion that we start to keep a diary of what happened, including all meetings and key points was something I took on board straightaway. Our friend also gave us a recommended order of actions to take and key people to contact in an escalating ladder of steps that helped us begin to take charge of our recovery. These included writing to our elected representative, approaching the Consumers' Association *Which?*, contacting the press with our story, and our ultimate recourse - the Financial Ombudsman's Service (FOS).[11]

---

9 I found out that they couldn't have taken any further amount as the daily limit of £25,000 transferrable was a limit on all accounts linked to an individual's unique ID with the bank.
10 Fuller details of this strategy can be found later in Part 2 Step 1.
11 For information on the Financial Ombudsman Service see: https://www.financial-ombudsman.org.uk/ (Accessed 17/02/2019)..

Tuesday 20th March – I called in on our bank manager to inform her we would be making an official complaint to the bank's own Complaints Resolution Service regarding what we saw as the failings of their text-stream and the deficiencies of their warning 12th March, the night before we were targeted. She noted the complaint and asked us to submit it in writing, which we did.

Wednesday 21st March – A representative from the bank's Complaints Resolution office rang to acknowledge receipt of our complaint. She informed me that a full investigation had been launched as a result of the seriousness of our fraud. She was aware that similar frauds had taken place using variants on the Amazon company name, such as PayPal. She also said she had needed to google the word "*smishing*" before ringing me to find out how the fraudsters do this, as she didn't know. She explained that there is a "weakness" in any smartphone whereby a fraudster, who knows what he/she is doing, can insert their own message into any given text-stream with the relevant tag such as OURBANK's own name. The smartphone's own functionality would look for the most appropriate "folder" (i.e. text-stream) to "file" that message under, thus making it appear to be from that source. The same infiltration can be carried out using any of the contacts on an individual's smartphone.[12] This left me wondering how I could be blamed for negligence when even OURBANK's officials seemed to know nothing about *smishing*?

Thursday 22nd March – 10:30am I submitted our formal complaint to our bank manager and posted a copy to the bank's Complaints Resolution office.

---

12 An interesting more recent development regarding the need to address this weakness in smartphones was announced in December 2018: a collaborative venture called PhishGuard from some of the largest telecoms providers in the UK to "stamp out a flaw in their systems that allows scammers to hijack text chains from a person's bank"; see the Which? article via the link: https://www.which.co.uk/news/2018/12/phone-companies-to-end-bank-text-scams/ (Accessed 17/02/2019).

The Fraud Team had still not contacted us. I also informed her we would delay going to the media until the following Monday to give the bank a couple of days to respond to our formal complaint.

OURBANK refuses to yield

We didn't have long to wait for the bank's verbal verdict. A couple of days later OURBANK's Regional Manager called and stated the bank's initial decision, having viewed our case, was to conclude that we had acted with "gross negligence". They would, therefore, not be covering our loss. Just under a month later we would receive in writing the bank's Complaints Resolution Team's formal response, confirming this.[13]

The battle is on

We now realised that we had a fight on our hands. We had to determine what was meant by "grossly negligent" and whether that did apply to us. Was the bank putting up a smoke screen, knowing full well that there were deficiencies in their own systems?

Traumatised as we were, the temptation was strong for us to give up right now, accept the bank's verdict and try to resume our lives, albeit £25,000 the poorer. We knew many people just accept what the banks say as being always correct. We had discovered that there was additional help available, from a body called the Financial Ombudsman Service that dealt with customer complaints against banks and businesses. At this stage, we really had no idea what this involved.

We did know instinctively that OURBANK could have done more to protect us, and that we probably had a case to argue. However, we had no real

---

[13] See Part Three for the relevant extracts from OURBANK's Complaints Resolution Team.

legal knowledge of the difference between "gross negligence" and "negligence" and needed to do some homework.

A key part of our defence, we felt from the outset, was the weakness of the bank's warning to us. The next chapter focuses on the bank's warning, what we felt were its inadequacies and our first line of counter-attack.

❖2

THE WARNING SIGNS

OURBANK's text-stream, as far as we had ever experienced it in the two years we had benefited from it, was safe, reliable, and a trustworthy source of information, warnings and advice. Never did we suspect it could be infiltrated.

It appears that five other customers in our area had fallen victim to this scam down the bank's text-stream before a warning went out from the bank on Monday 12th March, the night before our scam-text arrived on my phone. The warning that we received is included below (see Figure 2).

Monday 12th March at 19:37 - OURBANK's warning text came after work hours and I didn't see it until later when I was on my way to bed not really wanting to read anything on my phone. I skimmed it quickly, not really paying it much attention. As a result, I didn't comprehend the full import of what was happening. Its wording gave no clarity as to what the danger was, coming through this particular text-stream.

So the next morning when the fraudster's text came through, I did not connect this text back to the warning received. If anything I thought this was maybe another warning from the bank, rather than a scammer's hook. My awareness of the obvious current dangers in the cyber-world did not extend to the trick unfolding that was a *smishing* scam.

> Hi Jonathan. Fraud Warning. Fraudsters are currently targeting some customers via text message by adding their fraudulent message into the genuine **OURBANK** text stream. If you have clicked on a link or telephoned the **0330** number quoted and divulged any personal or account information please contact us. You do not need to contact us or take any action if you have not acted on or received the fraudulent text message. To unsubscribe from service texts, text **STOPSERV** to ………

Figure 2: OURBANK's fraud warning the night before (19:37 12/3/18)

We told OURBANK in our formal complaint how we thought they might have worded their warning better, as part of their duty of care to their customers. For example, a capitalised warning placed at the start such as: "THIS TEXT SERVICE HAS BEEN COMPROMISED" would have made a massive difference. We felt that the use of jargon didn't help. I had never heard or seen the words "text-stream" used together before. The text warning was overly long, and contained no capitals or exclamation marks to convey the seriousness of the threat. It was not alarming enough (unlike the Twitter feed, see Figure 3). We told them we get similar fraud warning messages from various quarters all the time, usually as an email. I just assumed that there was a general danger circulating, but nothing in the warning made me think that it would target this OURBANK's own text service.

We argued that the bank had made a mistake in not giving the same clear warning to all their customers that their Facebook and Twitter followers received. Who follows their bank on Facebook or Twitter? We certainly didn't. We, who were reliant only on the bank's SMS and emails, were not given the clear idea of the nature of the threat. No email was sent and the text above, of course, gives no clue as to the actual scaremongering lure the fraudsters were using. Figures 3 (i, ii, iii) below show the bank's Twitter feeds. Had we seen these I am convinced we would not have been duped.

Thread

OURBANK – 12/03/2018

Have you received an SMS message like this from **OURBANK**?

We're aware of a number of customers receiving these messages from individuals pretending to be **OURBANK**. Do not call the number.

Figure 3i

Thread

Today 12:49

OURBANK has noticed your debit card was recently used on 12-03-2018 12:45:43, at PAYPAL for 1749.00 GBP. If not you please urgently call fraud prevention on **0330** or Intl **+44330**. Do not reply by SMS

12/03/2018, 16:50

Figure 3ii

Thread

OURBANK

@OURBANK_UK

Remember – we'll never ask for personal information such as PINs, passwords or log on details over the phone, email or online. If you suspect fraud or attempted fraud on your account, please report it through our official channels, which can be found here ....

12/03/2018, 16:50

Tweet your reply:

Figure 3iii

Figures 3i, 3ii, 3iii: OURBANK's Twitter feed warnings 12/3/2018 at 16:50 (which came during working hours and nearly three hours earlier than the SMS text we received).

We didn't receive these clearer warnings as we did not follow OURBANK on Twitter. The originals on Twitter give a screenshot of the full text and the formatting that the fraudsters were using to deceive customers. There is also a clear instruction on their warnings not to ring this number. The warning we received, however, on the text stream merely said: "If you have clicked on a link or telephoned the **0330** number quoted and divulged any personal or account information please contact us" (see Figure 2 above).

What lessons can readers take from this? First and foremost, we all need to heed all warnings from our banks, the police, and other sources of information about the latest threats from fraudsters. It's very easy to become hardened to the fraud warnings and ignore them, thinking we know what the danger is, or that it will never happen to us.

We also need to put pressure on our banks to give us clearer, more up-to-date information about the latest threats from scammers, and to communicate this uniformly across ALL the platforms they use to communicate with their customers.

We need to be more suspicious of cold-callers

Some of us need to become much more suspicious of the cold-callers, emails and texts we regularly receive. We all need to keep up-to-date with the various threats whether on our doorsteps, by phone or online. There are also ways of blocking some of these threats.[14] Some useful information appears in the small print of the bank's Personal Banking

---

14 Which? The Consumers' Association provides useful, free, and up-to-date information and advice on the latest scams and how to protect yourself: https://campaigns.which.co.uk/scams-fraud-safeguard/ and https://whichcouk.bsd.net/page/s/which-scam-alerts.
See also https://www.which.co.uk/later-life-care/home-care/scams-and-older-people/common-online-scams-apwby4t6gp61 and https://www.which.co.uk/later-life-care/home-care/scams-and-older-people/understanding-online-scams-a51813g859kw (Accessed 20/7/2020). Fuller list is available in Appendix A.

guides, on the bank's website or social media sites. Unfortunately, most customers probably rarely, if ever, visit these.

Our banks and local police forces are getting better at flagging up the details of scams. If you are not sure what the implications are of a warning, ring or visit your bank to get clarity. In addition, it is a good idea to contact your local police force and to subscribe to their SMS texting service. These regularly warn of current activities of criminals in your area.

However, as the fraud world is a fast moving one that reacts to new technologies and moves on once the police and public get wise to the most recent one, we need to keep ourselves as up-to-date as we can so we can recognise a new threat when it comes.

Local newspapers can often also be a good source of information about recent threats at a given time, especially for those without access to the internet or a mobile phone.

Another good idea, for those on Facebook or Twitter, is to find your bank's Facebook page and/or Twitter feed. You can "like" the former and "follow" the latter to stay up-to-date with any alerts that may occur.

Convinced it was my bank

It didn't help that the fraudsters in our case started off with what are legitimate questions for banks to ask (such as my full name, date of birth and mother's maiden name)! It is appropriate for banks to ask for these particular questions. This approach did nothing to raise my suspicion.[15] Nevertheless to succeed in robbing me they, like every other scammer, still had to get me to part with the key information they needed – my security information and pin number.

---

15 Chapter 3 gives more detail on questions that a bank will NEVER ask customers as well as the difference of their questioning depending whether they call you or you call them.

Having convinced me they were bank employees, they led me to believe that the supposed Amazon purchase using my debit card was a genuine threat to be stopped immediately. To my ears, they were bringing a solution to that threat. I was convinced that they were from my bank with my best interests at heart.

The next chapter summarises all the lessons, in hindsight, to be taken from our experience thus far. Following that we will resume the narrative of our campaign to put pressure on the bank, and hopefully recover our money.

Hindsight Is a Wonderful Thing!

Hindsight is a wonderful thing.

In terms of the wording of the scammers' *smishing* text message, there were clues as to the reliability of the message that perhaps should have alerted me to what was happening.

Can you see the example of poor grammar ("if not you"), and one punctuation error (missing comma after "you")?

Also, banks will usually start their texts with the customer's first name – there was no "Hi Jonathan" at the start of that text.

I was told after the event by the Fraud Team that OURBANK no longer asks its customers to ring a number in the same text that they send to warn them.

I realised, again after the event, that "AMAZON ONLINE STORE" is not the usual format that confirmatory Amazon purchase texts use. It will usually read as "Amazon.com" or "Amazon.co.uk".

Individually, of course, none of these are proof of a scam text, but the absence of one's name (first or surname, or both) should make you more cautious. It may indicate a phishing scam duplicated across multiple mobile phone numbers or email addresses.

Note also that scammers may have obtained your full name from information publicly available (e.g. the phone book, or electoral register), so seeing your name mentioned isn't a guarantee that the text is genuine.

To click or not to click on a link?

I now never click on links or phone numbers, whether in a text or email, unless I am confident of the trustworthiness of my source. My bank says it now never asks customers to click even ones that appear in its own text-stream. That wasn't always the case, and we should have been alerted to this change in policy when it happened. Warnings against clicking on phone number links should now be a feature of a bank's standard warnings. I now have my bank's customer helpline number stored in my phone's contacts section, and I have it written down in a safe place. It can be found on the back of your bank card. It has also come to light that fraudsters are able to insert what looks to be one's own bank's security telephone number as a clickable link, but when the victim calls that number the call goes to a different number, the fraudster's own. I now always avoid tapping on clickable phone number links purporting to be from my bank, even when the number matches my bank's number!

I have resolved from now on to check with my bank directly if I am ever suspicious of an email, a text, or a cold-call purporting to be from them. This is as much about becoming savvy and thick-skinned towards cold-calls by phone (and on the door-step) as it is about wariness concerning SMS texts. We have now registered our landline and mobile phones with the TPS (Telephone Preference Service) system, which is free-of-charge. Most mobile phone and telecoms companies also have their own call-barring and anonymous caller reject service but not all of these are free. The TPS describes itself as "the UK's only official 'Do Not Call' register for landlines and mobile numbers. It allows people and businesses to opt out of unsolicited live sales and marketing calls".[16] The TPS can cut down on a lot of calls originating from the UK but it cannot guarantee to completely stop all UK calls, or callers from outside the country.

Sadly, there has even been a scam involving the TPS![17]

With hindsight, had I been unsure of anything, it would have been safest had I gone into my bank and talked face-to-face with an employee. I also learned, after the event, that if you choose to ring your bank to ask for advice in the immediate aftermath of a suspicious phone call, it is safest not to do so on the same phone. If fraudsters call you they will often advise you to ring a number but then they will stay on the phone. You may then dial what you think is your bank's number but end up talking to the same person who has just rung you, but who didn't hang up. Then you risk being duped into giving vital security details away.

We don't need to give all the above information to the genuine bank for them to see our account. Nor do we need the bank to view our online account in order to block a debit card. I only realised after the event that what "Tanya" was doing was persuading me, unwittingly, to allow her onto my account and then to facilitate the bigger transfer of money out of it.

---

[16] TPS (Telephone Preference Service) system website: https://www.tpsonline.org.uk/pages/what_is_tps (Accessed 07/02/2020).

[17] The fake Telephone Preference Service scam: https://www.saga.co.uk/magazine/money/spending/consumer-rights/the-fake-telephone-preference-service-scam (Accessed 27/05/2020). This scam involves fraudsters cold-calling victims, and falsely claiming to be from one of the well-known phone service providers. They then offer a paid-for TPS service - which they say is an "improved" version of TPS' call-blocking service - and ask for payment. Customers need to realise that once you register with the genuine TPS, companies are required by law not to cold-call you. Signing up to the TPS is free, and you'll never be asked for bank details.

I didn't authorise the transfer

At no point in the conversation did I knowingly authorise the transfer or the amount taken. These two points were crucial to our later official complaint to the bank and ultimately to the Financial Ombudsman. The threshold of "gross negligence" requires the customer to have approved the transaction and the amount. This is covered in greater detail in the second half of this book, which gives the "How to …" of our approach and the full wording of our official complaint against OURBANK.

Questions your bank will never ask you

Banks have to authenticate who you are *when you are ringing them*, as well as *when they are ringing you*, so it is vital to know what questions your bank will *NEVER* ask you, as well as what questions they *may* ask you in order to verify your identity. The questions asked will differ depending on *whether you are ringing them* or *they are ringing you*.

Nowadays the following mantra, or variants of it, is given repeatedly by our banks in their printed advice to customers and of course on fraud advice websites and police awareness leaflets: "Stay safe online and don't share personal information to unknown persons in email, online or by phone. Remember, xxxx Bank will *NEVER* contact you and ask you for your passcode, to move money to another account for 'security purposes', or to download remote access software to allow connection to your PC or mobile." Below are listed the kinds of questions the British Bankers' Association (since 2017 called UK Finance) state that a British bank would *NEVER* ask you. I now have these printed off and have them handy by the phone, and where I keep my security numbers. According to them, your bank would *NEVER*:

1. Ask for your full PIN number or any online banking passwords over the phone or via email.
2. Send someone to your home to collect cash, bank cards or anything else.
3. Ask you to email or text personal or banking information.
4. Send an email with a link to a page which asks you to enter your online banking log-in details.
5. Ask you to authorise the transfer of funds to a new account or hand over cash.
6. Call to advise you to buy diamonds, land or other commodities.
7. Ask you to carry out a test transaction online.
8. Provide banking services through any mobile apps other than the bank's official apps.

Questions your bank may need to ask you

However, the bank still has to ask you for some information to prove your identity. The actual information they *will* ask you for may differ from bank to bank, and from country to country. It is important to know what the relevant questions are that your bank will *need to ask you* to confirm your identity *when you are contacting them*. A definitive list of these questions is harder to get hold of, and banks, for security reasons, are reluctant to publish these questions.

- When your bank calls you: If it is your bank who rings you it will need you to verify who you are. Banks are probably reluctant to publish the questions they will ask you as they don't wish to give away too much that might assist fraudsters in adapting their approach. The key point to be aware of is that **if it is your bank on the other end of the line, and they have called you**, then they will be able to see your account without the need for you to divulge the password or security numbers that you use to access your online banking. All that your bank needs you to do is to prove your identity. Hence, they may ask you to give your full name, first line of your postal address, post code and date of birth. If they are calling you they won't ask you for your account number and sort code.

- *When you call your bank.* If it is you who calls your bank, then the employee will probably want to ask you what they call "account-related questions" – in other words the questions they ask will depend on what kind of account you are calling about. If it is about an account you have with them then they will probably ask you your sort code and account number, but they will never ask for your security number or passwords. If it is about a card they may ask you for the 16-digit number, but never for your expiry date or the 3-digit security number on the reverse of your card. They may also require you to give a telephone banking number and telephone banking password, neither of which allow access to your account, but merely confirm who you are. Some banks may have asked you when setting up your account to submit a memorable word. To check you know this they may ask you to give a couple of letters from this memorable word (e.g. the 2nd and the 4th, or the 1st and the 5th). They will not ask you for the full word. Some banks may require you to give your mother's maiden name or other security question that you will have also set up previously. If you don't have these ready to hand, then they may also ask you for a recent transaction or regular direct debit or standing order to help them confirm your identity.

Voice recognition is a recent valuable optional extra layer of security used by many banks.

Of course, a fraudster's biggest weapon is the fear that if you don't act swiftly you might lose a serious amount of money from your account. It is at this point you must keep your head and, above all, avoid giving the person at the other end the real information they need to genuinely get into your account! If you wish to ring your bank about a possibly fraudulent recent phone-call, you can safely call the relevant number on the back of your bank card or by using the contact details on the bank's website, preferably using a different phone to the one the suspicious call came on.

It is now time to return to the story and narrate how we gathered our resolve to make a fight of it, determined our plan, and then worked our plan.

Fighting Back, and Our Last Resort

Taking charge of your circumstances and fighting back are crucial when you have had a serious setback. For many there will be a strong temptation to give up hope of ever recovering your losses and to accept defeat.

A vital part of fighting back is to come up with a clear, achievable, and considered plan of action. Form a plan, then work the plan! Even if the plan doesn't lead ultimately to the recovery of one's losses or to only partial recovery, your physical and mental health and your closest relationships are even more important than your financial well-being. They deserve to be fought for.

Our lawyer friend had, from the outset, suggested some priorities for our battle-plan. We turned these into a sequence of actions to take and organisations to contact once we realised that OURBANK was not admitting any liability. In truth, he had suspected this would be the bank's likely tactic. First on our list was to contact was the Consumers' Association *Which?* They have long been standard-bearers in the UK for championing consumer rights.

Monday 26th March - We contacted the Consumers' Association *Which?* [18] via their Chat service. *Which?*

---
18 Consumers' Association Which? contact details: https://www.which.co.uk/about-which/contact-us (Accessed 19/02/2019).

Money Line quickly booked us a free call with an expert for the following week. We were impressed with the professionalism of "M.", the advisor assigned to us, and the personal interest he took in our case. He gave good advice on how to make a complaint, how to deal with the press and was willing to contact OURBANK to put pressure on them. His research into the archive of cases and rulings by the Financial Conduct Authority (FCA) and the FOS were vital to giving us the belief that we hadn't been grossly negligent. There were even previous favourable Ombudsman rulings in cases similar to our own.

"M.'s" advice was that the Bank had to prove "gross negligence" AND that we had "authorised the transaction" which, of course, we hadn't. We had only inadvertently allowed the fraudsters onto our account. At no time had we been consulted about the amount of the money transfer that the fraudsters were trying to take out of our account. The truth was we had no idea at all that fraudsters were in our account. We only found out the amount they had taken when I went online straight after the phone-call with the fraudster and found out what they had done.

Our bank's warning was inadequate

We had effectively been robbed, though not quite as one might be robbed on the street. Also "M." agreed the wording of the bank's text warning was inadequate, and said he thought it read a bit like a scam message itself. He warned us the bank would probably not change its position and that we should come back to him if this was the case. His intention was to then contact the bank himself and was hopeful they would agree to settle.

Dynamite! This discovery gave us reason to hope again. "M.'s" research revealed the limitations of banks' powers regarding "unauthorised" payments. Below is the full wording of his findings:

> Further to our phone conversation earlier today please find the information I mentioned:
>
> Financial Conduct Authority information about unauthorised transactions - https://www.fca.org.uk/consumers/unauthorised-payments-account
>
> It says: *Why a refund can be refused: Your bank can generally only refuse a refund for an unauthorised payment if:*
>
> • *It can prove you authorised the transaction – though your bank cannot simply say that use of your password, card or PIN conclusively proves you authorised a payment*
>
> • *It can prove you are at fault because you acted fraudulently or because you deliberately, or with "gross negligence", failed to protect the details of your card, PIN or password in a way that allowed the transaction*
>
> • *you told your bank about an unauthorised payment 13 months or more after the date it left your account, so make sure you contact the bank as soon as possible.*
>
> Financial Ombudsman complaints search tool - http://www.ombudsman-decisions.org.uk/

Figure 4 – Financial Conduct Authority information about unauthorised transactions

We now knew that OURBANK would have to prove we had authorised the transaction (i.e. the transfer of £25,000 out of the account). It couldn't simply say that the handing over of our password, card or PIN to the fraudster was sufficient proof we had authorised the payment which left our account. My hasty actions in phoning the 0330 number were carried out in all innocence, and purely to protect our account from the original, though of course fake, fraud of £2,499 that had never taken place.

Furthermore, "M." had clarified that the bank must "prove you are at fault because you acted fraudulently or because you deliberately, or with 'gross negligence', failed to protect the details of your card, PIN or password in a way that allowed the transaction". Clearly I hadn't acted fraudulently, and my failure to protect the details of my PIN and password had certainly not been deliberate. The issue was whether or not the handing over of my PIN and password had been grossly negligent. This presumably would be what a future ruling on our case would need to determine. In his opinion "M." did not think my mistake had wandered into the realms of "gross negligence". It might be regarded as careless, or perhaps negligent – but not grossly so!

Reinforcing our complaint

Full of anticipation of a turnaround in OURBANK's position, we sent in mid-April a follow-up letter to OURBANK's Complaints Resolution Team quoting the above information in its entirety.

Here is what we told OURBANK:

- At no point did we "authorise the payment" from our online account. We neither wanted to make the transfer nor did we authorise either the transfer, or the amount taken. We were victims of a scam.
- We did not deliberately or with "gross negligence" fail to protect the details of your card, PIN or password in a way that allowed the transaction. We acted in good faith and trust in OURBANK's text service that this was the genuine text service trying to help us prevent the theft of a smaller amount (£2,499) using our debit Card for an online Amazon purchase. We had been helped by the same text service before. We have pointed out clearly in our initial complaint document how we had been helped before by this service and how we were deceived by a totally believable scam.
- We should, therefore, be fully refunded for these reasons alone.

We have already pointed out our opinion that the wording and formatting of OURBANK's initial text warning was inadequate. The Which? Money

Line representative's initial reaction to reading our screenshot of OURBANK's own warning given on 12th March, the evening before the scam attack, was that "this reads like a scam text itself"!

OURBANK could have done more than it did to protect its customers once it knew that its text-stream had been compromised:

- It could have (temporarily) STOPPED ALL ONLINE TRANSACTIONS
- It could have (temporarily) STOPPED ALL ONLINE TRANSACTIONS above say £500
- It could have (temporarily) SUSPENDED ONLINE BANKING ACCESS
- It could have then temporarily advised customers to ring up the bank's own internet banking line if they wished to carry out transactions.

We were in control again! We were fighting back!

More good news!

"M." had continued to trawl through the vast archive of past rulings on the Financial Ombudsman's website [19] and had hunted down the case of "Mrs. J." – Case No. 116/9. In this instance the Ombudsman had upheld the case of a woman who, like me, had handed over the log-in details for her online banking account. In her case, she had used her phone's keypad to type in her PIN.[20] The key extract for us from this ruling, and from which we took great hope, was:

> "We looked carefully at the terms and conditions of Mrs. J.'s account, and we noted that unauthorised transactions would normally be covered by the bank. But the bank was saying

---

[19] The Financial Ombudsman's archive of past rulings is available at: http://www.ombudsman-decisions.org.uk/ (accessed 28/5/2020).
[20] Financial Ombudsman Service publications of ruling in Case No. 116/9 of Mrs. J.: https://www.financial-ombudsman.org.uk/files/2869/issue116.pdf (Accessed 21/04/2019). I have included in Part 2 (Step 1) the full wording of this ruling.

that this was a case of 'gross negligence'.

> The bank said that Mrs. J. should have known better than to disclose her log-in details and hand over her card. They pointed out that their online banking site, which Mrs. J. often used, warned people never to give out their full passwords – even to the bank. They also said that Mrs. J. should have read the security leaflet they'd sent her, which included some information on telephone scams.
>
> We took the bank's arguments into account. But we decided that although Mrs. J.'s actions had allowed the scammers to use her card fraudulently, she herself hadn't authorised the transactions."

This ruling tallied with the FCA's guidelines quoted above regarding transactions that the account holder hadn't actually authorised. This was similar to our case.

Armed with these reassurances we felt confident enough that we had a case to make that might influence the situation back in our favour, and could possibly be decisive should we need to resort to the Financial Ombudsman.

Aiming even higher

As time passed we realised that OURBANK wasn't going to reverse its decision any time soon. At this point we added an extra step to our action plan. This idea had come from our circle of friends and family. They suggested sending a formal letter to the OURBANK international Chief Executive Officer (CEO). The hope was that this would bring some pressure from above on our own country's CEO. We decided to omit asking for reimbursement of our lost funds. Instead, we would merely highlight what we felt were weaknesses in OURBANK's security systems for its private customers. So, on 29th April we submitted a letter to International CEO "Mr. B.", highlighting a ten-point list of weaknesses in OURBANK's security systems that we felt made it easier for the fraudsters.[21] One month later we received a non-committal response back from "Mr. B."'s Acting Head of Customer Service Delivery, thanking us for our letter and promising that our points would be considered.

Did this make a difference to our eventual outcome? We will never know but we believed at the time it was part of our pressure-building. It was a component of our decision to become vocal about our case. It was a factor in us staying in the driving seat of our fight-back. It restored our self-confidence.

But there was still more we could do!

More allies!

In the sequence of recommended steps, our lawyer friend had advised that, at some stage, we should contact our elected representatives and also the media. This should be done before submitting our case to the Financial Ombudsman. There was also the possibility of us having to consider the courts, but, in all honesty, we had no desire to do this. The Ombudsman would be our last resort, and only if the approach to the media and to our Member of Parliament (MP) led to nothing. Our desire was primarily to build pressure on the bank, who would be made aware of the media attention, were our story ever published. Also we were happy for what happened to us to make its way into the wider public domain to raise awareness and help prevent future such frauds. It would strongly encourage the banks to look again at their systems in the light of evolving scams, and to better inform and

---

[21] See Part 2, Step 7 for the main points of our letter to the International CEO of OURBANK.

protect their customers.

So our next step was to try and involve our Member of Parliament.

In May 2018 we wrote to our MP, "Mr. A.", to see if we could enlist his support in persuading OURBANK to cover our losses. "Mr. A." proved to be a great help, and we met with him on three occasions in his constituency office. Over the next four months he set up a meeting with the CEO of OURBANK, wrote to the Financial Ombudsman and also to the FCA. The Ombudsman took the unusual step of appointing a liaison officer to communicate with "Mr. A." regarding our case. We may never know what impact our MP's pressure had on persuading OURBANK to review our case and ultimately reverse its decision not to cover our loss. In hindsight, though, we believe that his intervention played a significant role in the turnaround of our story.

Going public

In early April 2018 we had seen a feature article in the *i-newspaper* telling the story of an email phishing fraud case in which the actress Elle Reams lost £10,000 but was later reimbursed by her bank. Encouraged by this, we decided to send our story to the *i-newspaper*. On Monday, 4th June 2018, it published our story as a full-page feature by Claudia Tanner entitled *"University lecturer conned out of £25,000 warns over scam texts that appear to come from banks"*.

In October 2018 a producer from Endemol-Shine, the production company behind the series *Ill-Gotten Gains*, approached us, having seen the afore-mentioned article on our fraud case in the *i-newspaper*. He wanted to interview us for their third series due out in 2019. They asked us to tell our story on camera with an emphasis on the impact the fraud attack had had on our lives. We found the interview to be difficult as we were obliged to revisit the painful memory of what had happened seven months earlier. It included a short role-playing of the incident with my laptop and mobile phone, a showing of the fraudster's texts as well as a discussion of how we had coped after the event. We were just keen to tell our story and our motive for going on camera was primarily to help the general public have a clearer understanding of how online banking fraudsters are operating in these days. The interview appeared on day-time TV across the UK on 10th July 2019 as part of Episode 13 of the third series on BBC1.

The TV programme was not due to be shown until after the reversal in our fortunes in December 2018, so it ultimately played no role in the bank's decision. However, we didn't know that at the time. We had also told ourselves that if all it did was help one or more individuals avoid being duped by the scammers then it would have been worth it.

In July 2018, four months after the scam, we took advice and decided the time had come to submit our case to the Financial Ombudsman Service – this was to be our last resort.

The FOS is a final referee or arbiter on financial disputes and complaints. Officially you have a six month window to contact them, after having formally talked to your bank about your situation and if you are still not happy with their response.[22] The service is free and decisions are usually final although individuals who are unhappy with a ruling have the option of the courts if they so wish. The UK is blessed to have such a body, as not every nation has one.

The FOS will initially attempt to resolve cases through their own investigators. Failing that they may choose to pass a case to their own independent

---

[22] Step-by-step process on how to submit a complaint to the FOS
https://www.financial-ombudsman.org.uk/consumers/how-to-complain
(Accessed 22/04/2019).

assessor. Each complainant is assigned a case handler. There is a two-stage process of assessments: the "initial assessment" and the "final binding assessment". If a complainant is unhappy with the case handler's initial conclusion(s), he/she may ask for an ombudsman to carry out a formal review of their case. The process is slightly different for financial businesses who have approached the FOS.[23]

In our case, our initial contact with the FOS was by phone to obtain their advice as to the best way to proceed. The adviser (based in London) at the other end of the phone was very helpful and explained the process clearly. He told us that, once we had submitted our formal complaint, he would process our application immediately into their "pool" and then assign us a case officer. He then assured us that as soon as we had submitted our formal complaint they would be contacting OURBANK. He warned us, however, that their backlog for decisions was around six months.

The whole process of drawing up our official complaint to submit to the Ombudsman was tiring and took some time, but we were confident it was worth doing. The FOS promise an initial response within 15 days to confirm receipt of a complaint, and this turned out to be the case.

On Tuesday 3rd July we submitted our complaint to the Financial Ombudsman Service by email. We were asked to attach documents relevant to our case. In our case we submitted seven attachments. These included the FOS Complaint form that we had completed and signed, an 11-page detailed summary of our complaint, screenshots of the *smishing* attack, our initial complaint against OURBANK, our supplementary complaint against OURBANK, and their official and final verdict on our case. Also

---

[23] For more information on the process see https://www.financial-ombudsman.org.uk/who-we-are/make-decisions (Accessed 22/04/2019).

we attached the FCA information on authorised/unauthorised transfers, negligence and the banks' burden of proof, and finally the FOS ruling 116/9 on behalf of and in favour of Mrs. J. on gross negligence vs negligence. As promised the FOS confirmed receipt within a fortnight. Then began the waiting game, which we were told could last six months. As it turned out we never did hear, or needed to hear, what the FOS's initial or final binding decision would have been, as our case was resolved just under six months later by OURBANK in advance of any decision that might have come from the Ombudsman. Thankfully!

The next chapter tells the story of how our nightmare ended – just in time for Christmas.

Jonathan Leakey

THE NIGHTMARE ENDS

It is another quiet Tuesday morning mid-December 2018. I am alone at home reading in my living room. Just over nine of the hardest months of our lives have elapsed since the *smishing* attack. Funnily enough, I am at this very moment, contemplating also how I would write the book of this episode in my life if we were ever to come out of it positively...

My phone rings. It's the same phone on which I received the *smishing* text back in March of the same year. Even now I still sometimes tense up when my phone rings, especially when I don't recognise the caller or when the "no Caller ID" is displayed.

In this case, it is clear who it is ringing me as the OURBANK Fraud team number is logged on my phone address book! This, too, is enough to cause me to tense up, wondering whether it is the bank wanting to bring some negative news regarding our case. Maybe they've heard from the Ombudsman and are just wanting to tell me they are still sticking to their original decision.

This is not why they were ringing. It is the bank's Customer Resolution Team leader calling with the news we had only dreamed of hearing, and many times had thought we would never hear.

"We have reviewed your case, and we have decided to refund your money, entirely."

There is a long pause as I take in what she has just said. My emotions are already leaping with the relief and joy of the news.

So much so, I hardly take in the rest of the message.

"Please know that this decision was taken independently of any decision the Ombudsman may have come up with."

What does the woman mean by that? Is it that the bank doesn't want us thinking our recourse to the FOS has influenced their decision? Is it that they want us to know that the bank was acting generously, of its own volition? Are they saying they haven't been pressurised by any argument of ours or of the Ombudsman's to reverse their prior decision? She doesn't tell us.

More to smile about

The good news does not end there. The bank's official continues,

"On top of that we have decided to compensate you with 8% of what you lost, on top of your refund, for the fact that you have not been able to benefit from having the money in your account these last nine months".

She adds that the bank is not willing "for sensitive reasons" to divulge the rationale behind this reversal of their original decision not to cover our loss. Again, we will never know what the "sensitive reasons" are influencing their decision. Maybe the committee is just feeling generous in the run-up to Christmas!

And at that moment, who are we to worry about their reasons?

I don't often cry, stiff upper lip upbringing and all that, but the tears I shed then are unrestrained tears of relief as the weight of the past nine months rolls off me, and the tension and heaviness, that had been my almost constant companion in that time, are lifted.

It is now time to ring my wife. She is in town doing some shopping. When she answers my call, I suggest she finds herself somewhere to sit or at least prop herself up as I have some news for her. I hear her squeal of delight as the news sinks in. I find out later she is in a queue at a checkout till, and that the lady in front gets the full story by way of release for my wife!

Over the next days we remembered our promise to our close family to throw a party if we ever recovered our money. It was also a very happy Christmas! We remembered our promise to each other to tell the story of our experience in order to open people's eyes to what online fraud can be like and its impact.

A knock at the door

One day early in January 2019, we received a knock on our door after this, from same local police officer who had so amazingly championed our case over the previous nine months. She had no idea that our case had been resolved favourably by OURBANK. Although she had managed to obtain a geographical address for the name we had submitted to her for the recipient "mule" account at Barclays, she had ultimately drawn a blank. She added that the authorities had decided a possible prosecution through the courts would not be possible. Both the National Fraud Intelligence Bureau (NFIB)[24] and Action Fraud had decided not

---

24 NFIB - the National Fraud Intelligence Bureau police unit in the United Kingdom is responsible for gathering and analysing intelligence relating to fraud and financially-motivated cyber-crime. The NFIB was created as part of the recommendations of the 2006 National Fraud Review, which also saw the formation of the National Fraud Authority. The

to pursue our case any further with the London Metropolitan Police as our reporting of the Payment Recipient's name had come three months after the event. The delay had been due to my reluctance to even go onto our online account after the trauma of our experience. Our police officer also told us that the man whose account had been used as the "mule" account, had himself reported three times to the police (and presumably Barclays Bank) that his account had, unwittingly, been used as a vehicle for fraudulent transfers!

Needless to say, the police officer who had come ready to console us, was soon sharing the joy of our turn-around. This was tempered only by the knowledge that, as far as we all knew, the fraudsters had got away with our money, even though OURBANK had decided to cover our loss and compensate us.

The fraudsters are still out there!

As I reach this point in the telling of our story, we are in the middle of the coronavirus crisis. The fraudsters, with their heartless cunning, are ever thinking up new ways of depriving innocent people of their hard-earned income.

The Consumers' Association *Which?*, on 31st March 2020, one week into the UK lockdown, cites the City of London Police's report of a 400% increase in scams as a result of coronavirus-related fraud.[25] The article lists a variety of devious, ingenious and cruel scams. These include phishing emails and texts. For example, one email circulating claims to come from the World Health Organisation:

NFIB was developed and is overseen by the City of London Police as part of its role as a national lead for economic crime investigation, and is funded by the Home Office. https://www.actionfraud.police.uk/what-is-national-fraud-intelligence-bureau (Accessed 27/04/2019).
25 Consumers' Association Which? article on early fraud scams during the Covid-19 crisis https://www.which.co.uk/news/2020/03/coronavirus-scams-how-to-spot-them-and-stop-them/ (Accessed 21/04/2020).

> "It's short and sweet, asking that you click on a link to what it says is a PDF offering advice on how to stay safe during the outbreak. ... If you click on that link ... it shows you a pop-up in front of what looks like the WHO's (World Health Organisation) actual website asking you to input your email address and password so that you can receive the non-existent PDF. Other phishing emails and SMS messages (known as 'smishing' texts) are also doing the rounds: Action Fraud has warned that emails purporting to be from organisations including the US Centres for Disease Control and the WHO are being sent with the aim of tricking you into opening malicious attachments or giving away your passwords."

The website lists other widely-circulated current scams such as fake lockdown fines, a fake *Her Majesty's Revenue and Customs* (HMRC) goodwill payment message, and a fake entitlement to free school meals designed to obtain your bank details. Furthermore, they document a fake WhatsApp requesting you to forward your "verification code" that could grant hackers full access to a person's WhatsApp messages, photos and videos.

Sadly, there will always be fraudsters, hackers, and thieves. Our hope is that in some small way we have contributed with our story to opening a few more people's eyes to the methods these people use and the damage they can inflict on innocent people, whatever their age or background. We also want to raise awareness to ways in which we can better protect ourselves.

Apart from stealing our money, there is often a wound inflicted by the fraudsters which is the trauma of the experience. For some people falling victim to a scam can go even deeper than the financial loss, and take longer to recover from.

The next chapter brings hope for those who, like us, suffered the emotional and mental trauma of serious fraud. There is healing available – from within, and from outside of ourselves. It can come from our own body's natural reserves of strengths and self-healing processes and from the circles of support and professional advice that is available.

Safe recovery from trauma is possible.

The practical steps we have outlined in our story above were an essential part of our recovery from trauma. For an outline summary of the *practical* steps that led, directly or indirectly, to us recovering our money, having been stung, please go to **Part Two** of this book which outlines our campaign strategy.

For resources and advice on how to protect yourself from fraud, and get practical help if you have fallen victim to a scam please refer to **Part Three** and the **Appendices**.

6

HEALING FROM THE TRAUMA

Definition of "traumatised" = severely shocked and upset in a way that causes lasting emotional pain (Cambridge Dictionary)

In the introduction to this book I quoted the findings of the Crime Survey for England and Wales 2015 which stated, "You are now 20 times more likely to be robbed while at your computer by a criminal based overseas than held up in the street".[26] I also said that "while being mugged on the street can be highly traumatic, getting 'cyber-mugged' can be equally traumatic, if not more so. While a victim of a cyber-crime will usually get away without any physical harm being inflicted on him or her, the experience often involves losing much more than the contents of their bank account, and will invariably leave emotional and psychological scars that can take years to heal".

In this chapter we want to highlight some pathways to healing for those who have, sadly, fallen victim to the fraudster's wiles and have been left emotionally and psychologically wounded as a result.

26 Daily Telegraph report on the findings of the Crime Survey for England and Wales (2015) https://www.telegraph.co.uk/news/2016/07/21/one-in-people-now-victims-of-cyber-crime/ (accessed 25/3/2019).

This chapter on healing and recovery is being written more than two years since we fell victim to the *smishing* attack that robbed us of £25,000 in an instant, and left my wife and me traumatised. I, Jonathan, was probably the more affected as I was the one who had been conned, who went through the steps of talking to the criminal and opened our account to let them make the fraudulent transfer. Just as a victim of burglary feels somehow his or her sacred space has been invaded and sullied, so also a victim of online fraud will feel somehow "slimed" by the cold hand of the intruder.

Lingering symptoms of trauma

While the reimbursing of our losses and the 8% compensation on top of that did much to heal the wounds, there is still some scarring left. What are the symptoms of this trauma and how do I know the scars are still there? In the immediate aftermath of the fraud the most frequent emotional and physical responses that I experienced were:

- Fear of visiting my online bank account.
- Anxiety at times when the mobile phone or landline rings.
- Anxiety when texts come in, especially ones from my bank.
- Dread about going online for credit card purchases or at a cash machine (ATM).
- Nervous reluctance to carry out online financial transactions (e.g. buying airline tickets, visiting Amazon, using PayPal, especially where these involve keying in a password, pin number or security number).
- Flash-backs where I relive the experience, moment by moment, trying to work out what I could and should have done differently.
- Self-chastisement, feeling foolish about what happened.

- Wanting to visualise who the fraudsters were, chase them down, and do damage to them!
- Fear of the future and the consequences of lack.

Do any of these symptoms remain even two years later? While most of the above wounds have healed, leaving just a little psychological "scar tissue", I can admit to unexpected flashbacks from time to time and the replaying of the experience in my head. Also, I still occasionally chastise myself. I sometimes feel the recurring fear of a repeat of the event and slight anxiety when a text comes in - especially one from my bank. I also still notice a feeling of reluctance and a slight dread, from time to time, when I go on my online account.

Is there a way through to complete freedom from the above? Yes, I believe there is, and we are well on the way there. The solution, I firmly believe, is a combination of practical steps, combined with a few well-advised internal disciplines and retraining of thought-patterns to counter the negatives.

The importance of making an early quality decision

It is vital to take a deliberate and conscious decision to rise up and overcome the trauma and scam stress. This should ideally happen immediately after the event or as soon as you feel able. It is wise to involve one or two trusted friends who agree to be your witnesses and "accountability partners" on your journey to recovery.

The most significant step my wife and I took from the outset was the refusal to succumb and assume we would never recover any of our money. This led us to formulate the practical steps we have chronicled so far in this book, and further developed in Part 2. We agreed to work a plan of action, with full awareness of our strengths and weaknesses, and to pursue it determinedly. This gave us something to focus on every day and a sense of progress whenever milestones were reached. We acknowledge that not everyone will recoup their lost money, and that therefore the journey to trauma recovery may be harder for them. Whether or not your money is refunded, however, the after-effects of the trauma of the attack may linger and impact negatively on your quality of life. Either way, we firmly believe there is a path through to healing for every victim.

There is a way through!

The good news is that, for all concerned, it is possible to come out the other side of your negative experience into wholeness, and a calm remembrance of what happened. For those who don't instinctively take steps that are restorative, there is much help on hand within one's own community of friendship and family, from experts in the field of trauma counselling, and from good, evidence-based video and book-based resources. Much about this journey comes as common sense. Before the era of the science behind psychotherapy, multiple generations of individuals and communities learned to heal through relying on their own inner resources and networks of support.

We can retrain our brains

It seems my wife and I instinctively did much that we see now is recommended as good practice by experts that we have read up on after the event. We attribute much of this to the help of our own circle of family and friends, as well as the resilience and hope that our Christian faith gave us.

Self-help can be useful, and indeed having inner motivation has to be a central part of any recovery path. One thing many therapists will agree on is the importance of taking charge of your own recovery.

Being aware of your own body's reactions, thoughts and emotions is an important first step. In other words, knowing yourself well will help you make good decisions in terms of a course of action, and being more accepting of yourself. For some, professional help from experienced trauma counselling may be valuable. This may be crucial for those who are struggling to access or benefit from their own inner resources or who lack a community of support.

Taking charge of your recovery!

In our case, by way of illustration, we decided that to sever our contact with OURBANK and to pursue a public assault on its reputation, would not help us internally, or help our cause. We would not be writing demanding letters to the bank's CEO or bitter letters to the press. We also decided early on that we would not go down the route of litigation.

Here, in no particular order, were the main steps that we took to take charge of our recovery.

- *Be kind to yourself.* It was important that I dealt early with the self-chastisement and self-reproach I felt at having been fooled. Being kind to yourself is vital, while of course at the same time learning the lessons so you don't repeat them! The bank's labelling of what I did as "gross negligence" was the hardest to deal with. Not letting that define my self-image and undermine my self-confidence was essential. I had to repeat to myself and believe "I am bigger than this one mistake" and focus on my strengths and successes in life. I reflected also that my relationships and circle of friends are worth so much more to me than my material wealth. I couldn't afford to wait until the verdict of "gross negligence" was overturned before I would feel better. From the outset I needed to be thinking in a healthy way. Of course, if the FOS had ruled that I had been grossly negligent it would have been even more important that I didn't let this define how

I regarded myself. For those who never recover their money, it may be even harder for the scars to heal. The lesson on being kind to yourself and some of the other advice from this chapter will be just as relevant, and probably more so, for these unfortunate people.

- It was important that we took *small, achievable steps* initially, which then gave us the confidence to take bolder steps after that. The easiest step was our decision to stay with our bank. This was accompanied by a determination to avoid thinking and speaking negatively about the bank. Our sending of a constructive letter (rather than a bitter and demanding one) to the International CEO of the bank was then a bigger leap that came out of these two previous steps.

- The decision to *keep a journal* was another small, achievable, daily step that helped us find that self-awareness and objectivity regarding our plight. It then provided a useful source of factual data that helped us with the more challenging tasks of writing letters to the press, agreeing to the media interview and contacting our elected representative.

- The choice to take, and even increase, *regular exercise* was a life-enhancing routine that got me out of myself and contributed to my morale on a daily basis. It helped that I already had a routine of taking regular walks in the countryside. In fact, my two or three walks a week became almost a daily event, alternating with visits to the gym. That hour or so of physical exertion, enjoying nature, feeling the wind, hearing the sound of the river and the birds, made a powerful difference to my mood each day, and remains my regular practice.

- *"Make lemonade from the bitter lemon."* Our adopting the inner posture of turning what had been a serious negative into the best positive we could, was of incalculable value in our emotional and psychological recovery. I have already outlined how developing a campaign strategy, or action plan, and then working that plan, helped us create momentum and a positive atmosphere around us.

We also promised ourselves and our family that if we won through to getting our money back we would throw a party. And that we did. We also determined that we would give a tenth of it away to our favourite charities. Looking back on the whole experience, it is these life-affirming actions that are now the dominant memories for us. These have overlaid the darker memories with a soft cushion of happy recollections. Writing this book has, I guess, been the ultimate aspect of living in the positive, or "making lemonade from the bitter lemon" that life had thrown our way.

Each person's path to healing will be unique to them

Recovery from trauma will, of course, differ from person to person, depending on the nature and degree of damage inflicted, on the make-up of each individual as well as their support base.

To take practical common sense steps and stick to them is often easier said than done! The successful pursuit and working out of any step-road to recovery in one's life requires an understanding that such a journey can be arduous and take time. Our testimony is that the effort was, and still is, definitely worth it.

The final section of this book is for all who want to raise their knowledge and vigilance levels.

In **Part Two** we outline the practical "campaigning steps" we took to recover our money, and then we give pointers to information on the many different scams encountered and the different resources and organisations available to help prevent fraud and help its victims.

We need to discern who our real enemy is (i.e. the fraudster), and understand the tricks he or she uses (many of them repeated, but often in fresh guises). Furthermore, we all need to know what help there is available both for the victim and for those seeking to protect themselves from falling victim. **Part Three** aims to provide guidance which will be helpful to these ends.

◆Part 2
HOW TO FIGHT BACK

LESSONS FROM OUR CAMPAIGN

STEP 1: DRAW UP A PLAN OF ACTION; WORK YOUR PLAN
STEP 2: KEEP A RECORD
STEP 3: IDENTIFY YOUR ALLIES AND BUILD A SUPPORT TEAM
STEP 4: DETERMINE THE PARAMETERS OF YOUR CASE
STEP 5: "GROSSLY NEGLIGENT", "NEGLIGENT" OR JUST CARELESS?
STEP 6: COMMUNICATE WELL WITH YOUR BANK
STEP 7: AIM HIGH!

❖ Step 1:

Draw Up a Plan of Action; Work Your Plan

For most victims of serious fraud, this is a massive assault on their whole being; their mind, emotions, will, and spirit. In all likelihood this fraudulent attack may well have negative effects on their physical wellbeing too, especially with the side effects of severe stress. The response will most likely be one of the three Fs; Freeze, Flight or Fight. Trauma can paralyse a person into inactivity and depression, or provoke a retreat or flight into oneself and into isolation. These usually solve nothing and can lead to cycles of negativity that can be harder to break the longer you leave it. For such people probably the hardest thing is to motivate themselves to take up the fight to attempt to recover their losses, or at the very least to conquer the trauma in pursuit of restoring their wellbeing and quality of life.

Our campaign cost us nothing in financial terms. We spent nothing on legal counsel, or therapy, but others may well be advised to invest something, if they can afford it, on getting help. However, our advice would be to look first at your own community of support, including your family, friends, colleagues, church or other community group, and if necessary your own GP or doctor, before going down the route of paying out money for help. You can also consult the range of excellent help available via the resources listed in the **Appendices** at the end of this book.

The choice to fight needs to be a deliberate, determined and well thought through process. Here is a summary of the key steps we took that worked for us. Every case is unique. Each individual's circumstances, support base and personality will differ and thus each person's strategy will, therefore, need to be tailored to suit.

The use of the term "fight" needs to be clarified. In our case, it wasn't about litigation, or taking a bitter and vindictive approach towards OURBANK. We decided to take the line of wanting to help the bank improve its systems and to point out clearly to their senior management and fraud team what we felt were the flaws in their systems. We decided to keep our accounts with the bank rather than to cut our ties. Each individual will need to make their own choices in this regard. Some may feel they wish to move their accounts to another bank if they feel their money would be safer elsewhere. Some may choose to go down the route of litigation which can be costly.

Our plan of action involved the following steps:[27]

- *Report of the crime to the police* to ensure that what happened to us was officially registered as a crime. The police then started looking into the crime.

- *Report of the scam to OURBANK,* and arrangement to meet our bank manager. We submitted our initial summary of what happened and initial complaint in writing to the bank. Our bank manager told us we had the option of submitting a formal complaint after this to OURBANK's Complaints Resolution Team.

---

27 Please note that none of these steps are prescriptive. These are just the steps we took to address our situation. Each victim of a scam will need to take considered and possibly professional advice as to which of these steps, if any, they take and in which order.

- *Submission of the formal complaint to the bank's Complaints Resolution Team.* Once our Regional Bank manager phoned us to say OURBANK had speedily and decisively declined to reimburse our money as, in their opinion, we had been "grossly negligent", we then submitted our formal complaint.

- *Involvement from a trusted support network.* In our case, we made contact with a retired lawyer friend, who in turn suggested the following further steps:

- *Contact with the Consumers' Association Which? –* While *Which?* does have a fee-paying legal advice service, you can request a free phone-call with a representative via the *Which? Money Helpline*. This advice proved very helpful in the following ways. He found FCA guidance and a FOS ruling that closely matched our own case and gave us hope that, if we ever went down the route of appealing to the FOS, we stood a reasonable chance of a ruling in our favour.

- *Letter to the International CEO of OURBANK* – not to demand reimbursement, nor to vent our anger, but to calmly point out where we felt the bank had let us down, and how they might improve their security systems going forward.

- *Meeting with the local elected representative.* This could, in the first instance, be a local councillor or your Member of Parliament. In our case, we chose to go straight to our MP. Again, this proved to be a fruitful decision as our MP proactively wrote to the FOS and FCA and then forwarded their replies to us. The FOS even went so far as to set up a specific liaison link between themselves and our MP concerning our case. Our MP also arranged a face-to-face meeting between OURBANK's CEO and himself. OURBANK wouldn't reveal the reasons for their review of our case nine months after the scam, but I have no doubt the pressure brought to bear by our MP through personal correspondence and this meeting will have played its part.

- *Contact with the press.* In our case this led to a full page in the UK's *i-newspaper* (May 2018). Five months later (October 2018), this article prompted a filmed interview with a TV production company. Our story was told in the *Ill-Gotten Gains* 2019 series. The newspaper article may have had an impact on the final outcome. The TV appearance won't have had a bearing on our outcome as it was shown only after we had had our money reimbursed. The recording took place before our turn-around, so we went into the interview as part of our campaign to raise awareness and, of course, build pressure on OURBANK. What clinched our decision to go to the press and to do the TV interview was our overriding motive to raise awareness and help individuals protect themselves from becoming victim. This motive and decision was part of taking charge of our recovery. The motive of building pressure was only secondary. We decided not to go down the route of telling our story in the local press, as we didn't like the idea of all our neighbours and the whole town knowing our story! In hindsight, we probably should have told our story in the local press as part of our desire to warn its readers of the dangers. After all, this had been an international criminal gang which had targeted people in our area. However, at the time, we just weren't ready for our story to be known so close to home.

- *Submission of our formal complaint to the Financial Ombudsman Service (FOS)* in London. Waiting times for such cases to be considered would be at least 12 weeks to six months. The Ombudsman ruling involves a two-stage decision process. An initial informal judgment is usually accepted by both sides in approximately nine out of ten cases. "But in around one in ten disputes, one or both sides use their right to 'appeal' to an ombudsman – who can use their official legal powers to make a final decision about how the complaint should be settled. Once the final decision has been made, our involvement is at an end – whether the consumer accepts the decision or not. No ombudsman, however senior, can overrule the decision of another ombudsman."[28]

We were still awaiting their ruling (six months after submission of our complaint to them) when OURBANK contacted us to say they had reviewed our case and had decided to reimburse us our loss and compensate us. We never received the FOS's verdict. This was because we didn't need to pursue it. On receipt of OURBANK's reimbursement we immediately cancelled our complaint with the FOS. Had we received a negative verdict from the FOS, we had the option of appealing this or taking OURBANK to court. We had decided before the event that, whatever the FOS's verdict, we wouldn't be taking this ultimate, and possibly costly, option.[29] Thankfully, we had no need to go down this channel.

Looking back, one step we failed to take in the early days after the scam was to summon up the courage to look at, and make a note of, the information on the transfer details on our emptied online account. At the time, I think I was too traumatised to even go into my online account, let alone explore the details of the transfer made. The online statement should tell you the name of the Payee and Payment Reference and the sort code and account number of the account the money was transferred to. This should be immediately reported to the police and placed on the victim's case area on the Action Fraud website. We only discovered nine months later that this may have prompted Action Fraud and the London Metropolitan Police to actively pursue an investigation into this mule account. Don't assume your bank's Fraud Team can see all this information, as one member of

---

[28] Financial Ombudsman guidance on their decision-making process: https://www.ombudsman-decisions.org.uk/final_decision.pdf (Accessed 15/03/2019).

[29] Consumers' Association Which? advice on recourse to the small claims court: https://www.which.co.uk/consumer-rights/advice/how-to-use-the-small-claims-court UK government website on making court claims: https://www.gov.uk/make-court-claim-for-money (Accessed 15/03/2019).

OURBANK's Fraud Team said on the phone that she could not see the Payee Reference details! You'd have thought this would have been visible to them!

❖ STEP 2:

KEEP A RECORD

Early on I was advised, by my lawyer friend and also the *Which?* representative, to keep a record of all the key events and dates of what happened, significant conversations and of any correspondence written or received. For some, keeping an audio recording may also help to process events but also one's emotions at each stage. My journal proved subsequently that this was indeed excellent advice. I was on top of each stage as it happened and could quote correspondence and times and dates whenever I needed to. It also assisted me in processing and externalising what I was going through. This journal was instrumental in getting me back into the driving seat of my life and taking charge of my recovery. In retrospect, it would have also been very useful at the time of the fraud to have had a device or app. to record incoming phone calls on my smartphone and our landline. This would have provided me with an exact audio record of the unfolding scam and of all subsequent conversations with the bank. A transcript of my conversation with the fraudster would have been a useful resource not just for myself but for those agencies researching and warning of the methods of fraudsters.

It is important to state that, following the implementation of GDPR (General Data Protection

Regulation) legislation in 2018 across the EU, there are new restrictions on the storage and sharing of data. In the UK, while it is legal to record phone calls, there are restrictions that apply, in particular in relation to consent, privacy and to the publicising or sharing of such data with third parties. Readers living in other nations need to comply with any laws that apply there to the recording of phone calls and to the sharing and publicising of such recordings.[30]

---

[30] Implications of GDPR legislation on recording phone calls in the EU and UK: https://www.ereceptionist.co.uk/blog/legal-to-record-phone-calls-uk (Accessed 23/8/2020).

❖ STEP 3:

IDENTIFY YOUR ALLIES AND BUILD A SUPPORT TEAM

"**D**on't get isolated and don't withdraw into yourself!" These were two pieces of advice that I was given early from a friend and which stayed with me. I am so grateful I heeded them. Most individuals have people around them who will probably form the most supportive and enduring circle of support. Money experts and therapists don't know you and may only be able to help from a distance. Their wisdom and guidance will no doubt be helpful, but we all also need emotional support, friends and daily encouragement. Our circle of support will drag us out of ourselves, help us keep our perspective, make us laugh and, if necessary, accompany us to meetings with elected representatives, the press and the bank.

The burden my wife and I bore during these nine months of our valley experience was, I know, more than halved by the network of friends, family and advice that came together around us during that period. First of all, my wife and I had each other and we needed to be together in spirit and work together. My wife could have blamed me for my having been duped but she didn't. This stopped me from indulging in the self-reproach I felt for having allowed myself to be unwittingly conned.

We all need people around us who will be accepting, forgiving, and encouraging. They will be firm with us from time to time and will help us resume the fight when we feel like giving up. Trauma and self-reproach will want to isolate and muzzle you. You have to seek out your allies at such times; those on whose shoulders you can cry. You can share your negative feelings, whatever they might be. One can have feelings of self-chiding, despair, frustration, and rage. Having such a support network played a large part in us taking full charge of our recovery.

Our wider circle of support, beyond our friends and family, came from the experts and advocates we chose to go to for advice and support: a retired lawyer, our MP, a journalist who we knew was championing victims like ourselves in her articles, money experts and advisers. We even found an unexpected ally in the local police officer who took our case to heart and went well beyond the call of duty to help us. We made sure, after it was all over, to send a letter to her commanding officer honouring her for her help. Likewise we also took time to thank the others who had helped us. It is also important to remember to keep your allies posted on any significant developments, breakthroughs or reversals.

◆ Step 4:

Determine the Parameters of Your Case

Early on you need to find out if you actually have a case; a cause to fight for in terms of going after recompense and even compensation. It's vital not to meekly accept what your bank would like you to believe. They will want to avoid having to cover your loss and also having to pay you compensation. Banks have a track record of "blaming the victim". An article in *The Times*, dated 22nd August 2018, and entitled "*Stop accusing fraud victims, banks told*" chides banks who blame victims of fraud. They make the point (that was so true in our case) that most banks will want to make you believe you were "grossly negligent" and to give up the fight. However, as the article suggests, the tide of official opinion is turning. It had begun to change during the time we were battling our case. The article cites the criticism by the Financial Ombudsman of banks for "wrongly accusing customers of negligence after falling victim to a scam when they have been merely careless".[31]

---
31 Times article (22-08-2018) attacking banks who blame victims of fraud. https://www.thetimes.co.uk/article/stop-accusing-fraud-victims-banks-told-hnd5f7tvj#:~:text=The%20ombudsman%20says%20that%20banks,executive%20of%20the%20ombudsman%2C%20said

For those who have fallen victim to Authorised Push Payment (APP) fraud, a very different scam to the one we fell foul of, the tide is also turning in the UK. *The Consumers' Association Which?* has been fighting a long-running battle with the UK banks and with the UK Government to help victims of such scams. An APP scam, also known as a bank transfer scam, occurs when a person unwittingly transfers money from one's own bank account to one belonging to a scammer. A recent (2019) example of an APP scam can be found on *The Consumers' Association Which?* website. The article explains what happened and how the victim's bank initially tried to avoid its responsibilities to the new code. Below is an extract from the article which is worth reading in full:

> "Criminals stole £30,000 from a vulnerable 89-year-old customer in a sophisticated and drawn-out impersonation scam. Her bank, Lloyds, initially refused to reimburse these losses, despite being signed up to a voluntary code that has introduced significant new protection for fraud victims. Reports of authorised push payment (APP) fraud – where the victim is tricked into moving the money into a scammer's account – jumped by 45% in 2019 and resulted in losses of £456 million. Most payments are made via online banking, but there has been a 177% spike in APP scams initiated via mobile banking apps and a 40% spike in those started in branches."[32]

So, a little research into the bigger picture relating to the type of scam you have fallen victim to is crucial and may well bring hope that there are laws, regulations or FCA and FOS rulings that might require one's bank to act in a certain way with regard to your case. This, in turn, will help you set the parameters of your position and correspondence with your bank,

---

32 Example of a 2019 APP scam https://www.which.co.uk/news/2020/06/scammers-pose-as-the-national-crime-agency-to-steal-30000-from-lloyds-customer/

the press, your locally elected representative and ultimately the Financial Ombudsman or any litigation you may choose to pursue.

It is worthwhile to have a good think and decide early on what position you'll take with your bank – whether to stay with your bank and adopt the route we took, or to cut one's ties. Reasons for the latter may be the need for a bank with possibly better security systems.

❖Step 5:

Be Clear

Were you "grossly negligent"?

My strongest conviction is that we ultimately won our case by demonstrating to all concerned that I had not been grossly negligent in allowing the fraudster to access our account. Getting clarity on the definition of "negligence" and "gross negligence" was essential. Our ally "M." of the Consumers' Association *Which?* had carried out incisive research and found the significant ruling by the Financial Conduct Authority giving information about unauthorised transactions. That ruling bears repetition here. It states:

"*Why a refund can be refused*: Your bank can generally only refuse a refund for an unauthorised payment if:

- It can prove you authorised the transaction – though your bank cannot simply say that use of your password, card or PIN conclusively proves you authorised a payment.

- It can prove you are at fault because you acted fraudulently or because you deliberately, or with 'gross negligence', failed to protect the details of your card, PIN or password in a way that allowed the transaction."[33]

To back this up "M." also hunted through the large inventory of cases and rulings by the Financial Ombudsman Service. Using the Financial Ombudsman complaints search tool[34] he tracked down the ruling 116/9 on the case of "Mrs. J."

The Financial Ombudsman Service ruling on "gross negligence vs negligence"

The following extract is the FOS account of and ruling on the case of "Mrs. J."

116/9 - consumer complains that bank won't refund her money after she gives scammers her card and bank details

> Mrs. J. received a phone call from her bank to tell her that her card had been cloned - and that she should ring another department at the bank immediately.
>
> Mrs. J. put the phone down and rang the number on the back of her debit card. The person she spoke to asked her the usual security questions before they would discuss anything with her.
>
> Mrs. J. was then asked to give some more details - including the log-in details for her online banking account - and to type her PIN into her phone's keypad. Once she'd done this, the person on the line told Mrs. J. that they were sending a courier to pick up her existing card, and that a replacement would be sent out within five working days. Mrs. J. did everything she was asked to do, and the courier collected her card later that day.
>
> But after three days Mrs. J. started to get worried.

---

[33] Ruling by the Financial Conduct Authority: https://www.fca.org.uk/consumers/unauthorised-payments-account (Accessed 21/04/2020).
[34] Financial Ombudsman archive of decisions: http://www.ombudsman-decisions.org.uk/ (Accessed 21/04/2020).

She hadn't received a new card and nobody from the bank had contacted her. So she checked her account online, and saw that several large transactions had been made.

She realised that she had probably been the victim of a scam.

She got in touch with her bank and asked them to get the money back. But the bank said that they weren't responsible for what had happened – and that Mrs. J. hadn't taken care of her security details. They refused to refund the money.

Mrs. J. complained, but the bank refused to reconsider. So Mrs. J. decided to refer her complaint to us.

Complaint upheld

We looked carefully at the terms and conditions of Mrs. J.'s account, and we noted that unauthorised transactions would normally be covered by the bank. But the bank was saying that this was a case of "gross negligence".

The bank said that Mrs. J. should have known better than to disclose her log-in details and hand over her card. They pointed out that their online banking site, which Mrs. J. often used, warned people never to give out their full passwords – even to the bank. They also said that Mrs. J. should have read the security leaflet they'd sent her, which included some information on telephone scams.

We took the bank's arguments into account. But we decided that although Mrs. J.'s actions had allowed the scammers to use her card fraudulently, she herself hadn't authorised the transactions.

The person who had called Mrs. J. had stressed the

urgency of the situation – and that she needed to act to make sure her account and card were safe. Mrs. J. had phoned the number she believed to be her bank's immediately. The conversation had started with security questions, so Mrs. J. had had no reason to think that anything was wrong.

Taking everything into account, we took the view that Mrs. J. hadn't acted in a grossly negligent way. And we were satisfied that she clearly hadn't authorised the transactions herself. In these circumstances, we told the bank to refund her all the money in question.[35]

This FOS ruling gave us real hope that our case was similar and that our outcome might be as positive.

---

35 FOS web-link giving the ruling on the case of "Mrs. J." https://www.financial-ombudsman.org.uk/files/2869/issue116.pdf#cs1 (Accessed 21/04/2018) – the italics are mine.

◆ Step 6:

Communicate Well with Your Bank

Having submitted our initial formal complaint to the bank, we didn't have long to wait to hear back from someone senior in the bank. Ten days exactly from the scam, my diary entry for the 23rd March reads:

OURBANK's case against us, formulated within a week of our initial letter of complaint, was built on the main premise that we had been grossly negligent. Below were further points they made to defend their position:

1. The bank's text-stream wasn't actually *hacked*, as I had originally thought. The fraudsters are able to infiltrate a bank's (or any named text-stream) and fool our smartphones, and us, into thinking their texts have come from the authentic source. It soon became clear that OURBANK did know something about *smishing*; it had been in the public domain for a while, but we were left wondering why OURBANK hadn't let its customers know about this specific threat. *Which?* for example had highlighted the danger on 4/11/2017: https://conversation.which.co.uk/money/scam-text-message-from-bank/#more-102655

2. They told us that they, OURBANK, couldn't close down the text-stream coming to us as it had to be done from the customer's end (via the "**STOP**" link at the bottom of each text received from the bank). They stated that we could have closed it down at any time. From our perspective, up until then we didn't know of *smishing* and the possibility of fraudsters infiltrating messages in this way. Why would we want to close down what, up until then, had been a service that had only helped us?

3. OURBANK's view was that because we had given out our three-step security details we had infringed the bank's Terms and Conditions. In our defence, we felt the bank had not fulfilled its duty of care to us its customers to ensure that its SMS stream was fraud-proof. We reiterate our point that the wording of their advance warning, at least to those relying on the SMS "stream" alone, lacked clarity as to exactly what the threat was and where it was coming from. We also felt we had a right to have received the same quality of warning by text that we found out later the bank's Twitter and Facebook users were privy to. Also, why did we receive nothing by email to reinforce it?

We realised that, if we wanted to stand a chance of OURBANK reimbursing us our loss, we would need to make an official complaint to the bank's own Customer Resolution team, as the first step in the complaints process that would ultimately lead to the Ombudsman.

Below are the key elements of our formal complaint to OURBANK. There are various template letters available online to help customers write to their bank. For example, the Consumers' Association *Which?* provides a sample template letter for individuals to adapt and expand upon by way of an appeal to their bank to cover their losses in the event of an email *phishing* scam.[36]

We were advised by the *Which?* representative to write a fuller letter of complaint outlining exactly what had happened. This would explain why we were disagreeing with the intransigent stance being taken by OURBANK and with their accusation of gross negligence on our part. The letter would also outline why we felt the bank's warnings had been inadequate in our case.

Below is the full letter of our complaint to OURBANK. The bank would, within 20 days, reject our complaint, and we would then face the decision as to whether or not to increase the pressure of our campaign to the next degree:

> **COMPLAINT TO xxxx BANK**
> **From**: Dr and Mrs Jonathan and Patricia Leakey
> **Bank account number:** xxxxxxxxxxxxx
> **PSNI Crime Reference:** xxxxxxxxxxxxxxxxxx.
> **National Crime Reference Number/Action Fraud reference:** FRCxxxxxxxxxxxxxxxxxxxxxxx
> **Date committed:** Tuesday 13th March 2018
> **Time:** between 11:36am and 12:10pm.
>
> We are writing to formally issue our complaint at what we deem to have been negligence by xxxx BANK on two matters, which led indirectly to us being defrauded of £25,000 last week:
>
> 1. The inadequately worded fraud alert sent out on xxxx BANK's text-stream service on 12th March 2018 – *see Figure 2 above*. (NB xxxx BANK's Twitter feed warnings, of which there were TWO on the same Monday 12th, which I have only viewed since the fraud as we don't use Twitter much and weren't "following" xxxx BANK, were much clearer and less ambiguous communications (*see Figure 3 above*), and might have saved us had we seen it). The text warning

---

36 Sample template for wording a letter to your bank, supplied by the Consumer Association Which?: https://www.which.co.uk/consumer-rights/letter/letter-to-your-bank-if-you-have-been-the-victim-of-a-phishing-scam (accessed 22/5/2019).

that appeared the day after the event was much clearer but still didn't admit that the text-streaming service had been compromised/hacked). As for the warning on xxxx BANK's online e-banking site I hadn't been on my account for a while and so had not seen the warning there. I only saw the online warning, whose wording was equally poorly worded and has since been removed, when I went online to check the account after I had spoken to the fraudster.

I explain in detail below why we deem the wording of the text-stream warning to have been inadequate. I am a linguist and a university lecturer with a doctoral thesis in my subject; as such I am well aware of the importance of precise wording, and how poorly worded text can seriously hinder communication. I am also the Neighbourhood Watch officer for my street and take time to issue warnings to our neighbours about scams (such as the HMRC one) that up until now have either come through door-step salesmen, hoax emails, or texts out of the blue. Never did we suspect the bank's own in-house alert service to be compromised

2. The fact that xxxx BANK did not close down the text-streaming service immediately once they knew it had been compromised. xxxx BANK were obviously aware of the scam before the 12/3/18 message, which was why they put out the warning. This omission alone put their customers' money at risk.

We put our trust in xxxx BANK's text-stream service as it had warned us successfully on June 28th 2017, with a warning not too dissimilar from the one the fraudsters used last week, to protect us genuinely from what they believed may have been an attempted fraud using our Debit card number. This was the very first message we ever received on the text service. It, too, had advised us to telephone a number that was given at the bottom of the very same text; this is evidence that xxxx BANK does put a number on their warning texts. So, when the scam text appeared on 13/3 warning us of £2,499 money being spent off our new Debit card on Amazon the desire to stop what we only now know was a "fake fraud" designed to gain our trust, immediately compelled me to want to take rapid action, and ultimately hand over access to our online account. I only did this after I had reassured myself by checking back up the xxxx BANK text-stream on my phone to see previous genuine messages from xxxx BANK. This reassured me that the scam text was genuine and reliable.

HAD xxxx BANK's TEXT SERVICE NOT BEEN IN EXISTENCE WE WOULD NOT HAVE FALLEN VICTIM TO THIS FRAUD. If the money is not recovered from the criminals' own bank accounts, we expect, in light of xxxx BANK's negligence, as we demonstrate in this letter, with regard to the management of its text feed, **to receive full recompense swiftly of our loss from xxxx BANK itself.** We also would like to be reassured that xxxx BANK is taking measures to secure its texting service, for the sake of all its customers.

xxxx BANK's inadequate text warning 12/3/2018 (see *Figure 2 above*):

19:37 Monday night (12th March), the warning text came through. There was nothing in its wording to make me believe that this very text service was compromised. I was in a rush between jobs and only scanned the first few lines. There was nothing in the first few lines to say THIS TEXT-STREAM has been compromised. There were significant failings in the message:

- **It was not at all clear that it was xxxx BANK's very own text service I was looking at that was compromised.**

- A capitalised warning placed at the start such as: **"THIS TEXT SERVICE HAS BEEN COMPROMISED/ HACKED"** would have made a massive difference.

- **Use of jargon**: "text-stream" – I had never heard these words used together before.

- It was **too long**, and contained **no capitals or exclamation marks**. It was not alarming enough (unlike the Twitter feed). We get similar messages from various quarters all the time. I just assumed that something similar might come my FROM ANOTHER SOURCE, but not from xxxx BANK's own text service.

> – xxxx BANK's Twitter followers, of which I wasn't one, got a MUCH CLEARER SERVICE on Monday 12th March (see *Figure 3* above). I am not a regular Twitter user by any means and was not following xxxx BANK.
>
> [*The remainder of this complaint letter then included the various screenshots from my phone that feature in previous sections of this book, and for which I have included references in the complaint letter*]

Figure 5 – the full letter of our complaint to OURBANK – April 2018.

We made sure that we followed OURBANK's procedure for making official complaints. This procedure was explained clearly online and the bank promised that "if we have not resolved your complaint by the close of business on the third business day after we receive your complaint, we will send you a letter acknowledging your complaint. This letter may also include our final response to your complaint. If we need more time to investigate your complaint, we will keep you informed of the steps we are taking to deal with it". In our case the bank replied with its official report dated 4th April, which was within the promised 20 days.

Below (Figure 6) is an excerpt from OURBANK's formal response to our complaint, dated 4th April 2018:

> The bank considers that the fraud warning issued by the bank on 12th March 2018 was an adequate warning to its customers to be on the alert for fraudulent text messages and you have acknowledged that you did receive the warning. Furthermore, if you had not disclosed your online security details to the fraudsters then the payment would not have been made from your account. Accordingly, I am satisfied that the bank did not do anything wrong in this regard to this matter.
>
> In summary, the bank is not obliged to provide you with a refund under the account terms and conditions as we consider that you were grossly negligent when you shared your online personalised security details and you failed to observe the fraud warnings issued by

the bank.

As soon as we became aware of your actions, we suspended your eBanking agreement and, referred the matter to our Fraud Team. Our records indicate that you called us at 12:15 pm on the 13th March and following this call our Fraud Team were alerted. They confirm that Barclays were contacted at 12:29 pm on the 13th March and were advised that no funds remained in the receiving account.

We are aware that you received a text message previously (from us) about the use of your debit card – you will note, however, that the contact telephone number in the genuine text from the bank begins XXXXX. Furthermore, when you contacted us to discuss the text, we did not ask you to divulge your personalised security details and as per our recent messages, and fraud warnings, this is not something we would ever do.

Finally, we note you consider that the bank could have taken additional steps to protect its customers but we remain of the view that the fraud alert was the appropriate and proportionate step to take in response to the fraud risk. We are still satisfied the fraud warning was suitable and we are not aware of any other such in the incident after the alert was issued on 12th March 2018.

Figure 6 – excerpt from OURBANK's formal response to our complaint, dated 4th April 2018

At this stage, one month into our nine month journey, things weren't looking very hopeful. We now knew we were faced with two choices. On the one hand we could give up the fight, assuming that the bank was never going to change their mind in the face of us who, in their eyes, were just two customers amongst thousands.

Alternatively, we could steel ourselves for the fight and continue in the hope that somehow we could generate some momentum on our behalf that might just turn things around for us. This was the route we opted for, with no idea how long it would take or whether we would meet with success at all. We really felt we had no choice: we had lost too much to give up at this stage. So, what were our next moves?

◆ Step 7:

Aim High!

In addition to this official complaint to the bank, and as a result of the negative response from within its regional complaints resolution system, we decided to write to the International CEO, "Mr B." of OURBANK. We submitted this letter on 29th April and one month later we received a response from OURBANK. We decided that we would merely highlight what we felt were weaknesses in OURBANK's security systems for its private customers. In our letter we listed ten points where we felt the bank could improve its security systems with regard to its personal banking arrangements.

Banks differ with regard to procedures for checking identities by phone. These include the ability to customise accounts online, key numbers, PIN-sentry gadgets and two-factor authorisation of transactions. Here is an abridged version of the main points we raised with OURBANK's International CEO. This will encourage you to make sure that you carry out adequate research, preferably in advance of committing to a certain bank. You need to know what your bank's security procedures are as they apply to its ordinary customers.

- Banks should inform their customers promptly and on all their channels of communication with their customers as to the exact nature of *smishing* attacks, and indeed any new threat from fraudsters. We had never been informed by OURBANK about *smishing*, even though we have found out subsequently that information has been in the public domain since as far back as 2009. Customers need to give informed consent, fully aware of the risks of *smishing* when they sign up to receiving SMS texts. It is the responsibility of organisations to ensure their communications to its customers are clear, precise, unambiguous and jargon-free. Anybody who reads such communications should be in no doubt as to the nature of the message. The text warning we received from the bank was overlong, used jargon, and did not make it clear that the very SMS I was reading had itself been compromised.

- Banks should immediately block telephone numbers they suspect of fraud and not wait 24 hours or more. In our case, OURBANK clearly knew the 0330 number was fraudulent as it was mentioned in the warning text. Why did they not then immediately have it blocked? There are three ways banks can request blocking of numbers; through the telephone number provider, the police or the National Fraud Intelligence Bureau.

- Banks should all adopt a PIN-Sentry type gadget similar to that used by other banks such as Barclays for secure accessing of online accounts.[37] This would, I am certain, have made me think much harder before divulging crucial security information.

- Banks should allow their customers to set a threshold for the maximum size of transfers possible within a 24-hour period from one's online account. We would never have accepted a £25,000 limit as we never make online transfers of such a size. We suggest that any transfers of amounts higher than £5000 should require the customer to go in person to their branch to authorise it. At least, customers should be given the option to request this.

---

37 Examples of the Barclays PIN-Sentry can be seen here. These now include audio accessible PIN-Sentries and mobile PIN-Sentries: https://www.google.co.uk/search?q=barclays+pinsentry

- Banks should introduce two-factor authentication as mandatory for every transfer out of an online account. There should be an option to request a six-digit code sent as a text to your mobile phone, as happens with online purchases.

- All banks should allow customers to request that any sub-accounts be invisible online. This would ensure that fraudsters, if they ever gained access to one's online banking, wouldn't see all the information in your accounts.

- Banks should be required to publish a clear list not just of the "account-related questions" that their employees would ask you if you were phoning your bank, and how these might differ from the questions the bank would need to ask you if they were ringing you (such as date of birth, address and post-code). In addition, it is important to highlight the questions they would never ask. Customers know they have to divulge certain information and some, such as those who are elderly, may easily get confused.

- Banks should cooperate more closely with each other to prevent fraudsters being able to quickly transfer money to and from "mule" accounts to ensure that stolen money isn't traceable. If there had been, say, a 24-hour delay (for inter-bank security checking) between our money being instructed to leave our account and going into the "mule" account at Barclays, our loss might possibly have been recoverable.

We did not have any high expectation that this letter would lead directly to any reimbursement. We were committed to ensuring that, at the highest levels, OURBANK knew about our case, knew that we were determined to keep up the pressure on them and highlight the deficiencies, as we saw them, of their systems. We reassured them we were loyal customers of the bank, and had no immediate intention of switching to a different bank. We wanted to give them no excuse to stop dealing with us and we had made it clear, at least to the bank's regional officials we spoke to, that we were going to take our case to our elected representatives and the media too.

The reply we received (see Figure 7 below) came from "Mr. B."'s Acting Head of Customer Service Delivery, "Mr. C.". Below is the reply from "Mr. C." dated 30th May 2018:

> Thank you for your letter dated 29th April addressed to Mr. B... which has been passed to our capital Global Fraud department for attention.
>
> We understand that you recently fell victim to a most cruel scam in which you were tricked into revealing your confidential eBanking log-on credentials. We also understand that, unfortunately, our efforts to recover any funds from the beneficiary account which received the resultant payment have not been successful. We believe that this outcome has already been conveyed to you and that our Customer Resolution Team in OURBANK have also provided you with details of the Financial Ombudsman Service.
>
> You have expressed in your letter ten specific open brackets "lessons" regarding this unfortunate experience and which describe what you perceive to be deficiencies in OURBANK systems.
>
> We would like to assure you that we do take on board customer comments and feedback and thank you for taking the time to detail these. As I am sure you will be you will appreciate, we are unable to discuss the detail of our existing and planned fraud and security controls with either customers or third parties as they must be treated with the utmost degree of confidentiality.
>
> We take the prevention of fraud seriously and we constantly review the fraud mitigations we have in place and regularly update them to take cognizance of new and emerging threats. We acknowledge that our customers can also play a vital role in the prevention of fraud, in particular, by taking extreme care with sensitive information such as Personal Identification Number (PINs) and the likes.
>
> We note that you are long-standing customers of this bank and we are hopeful that, despite these most

> unfortunate circumstances, you will continue to have a relationship with us in the future.

Figure 7: Letter from "Mr. C.", OURBANK's international Acting Head of Customer Service Delivery – 30/5/2018

It is impossible for us to tell whether our letter had any direct impact on our eventual resolution. As "Mr. C." made clear in his letter above, he could not for reasons of the confidentiality of their own security systems let us know what action they intended to take as a result of our letter to their international CEO. We may never know of any changes to actual security and practice on the bank's part that may have been made as a direct result of our letter.

Nevertheless, since our fraud case we have become aware of a number of improvements to OURBANK's warnings and information to existing customers, such as the guidance on fraud-prevention and awareness on their website and in their mailings to personal banking customers. Interestingly, the case given on its website of a *smishing* fraud uses the example of the March 2018 fraud to which we fell victim.

In 2019 OURBANK did away with the plastic card with multiple key numbers that I was using at the time of our fraud. In 2019 it introduced its own version of the PIN-sentry that we believe is an improvement and a tightening of its security procedures for online banking.

OURBANK may well, also, have registered with the *Phishguard* initiative taken by leading telecoms companies set up in order for the banks to protect their sender ID, and thereby hopefully put a stop to the kind of *smishing* attack such as we encountered.

Further improvements OURBANK has made to its security arrangements since March 2018 include the following:

- New information and clearer warnings on the bank's website and personal banking booklets regarding *smishing* and other fraud types.

- After 7th December 2019 customers have no longer been able to log on to eBanking using their Access ID security card. An OURBANK ID app. has replaced the security card which was a credit card-shaped card with scores of six-digit single-use security codes.
- An "eSafe ID" device, similar to Barclays PIN-Sentry, which generates the codes that customers previously would have got from their security card. We believe that this improvement may make some customers think twice before divulging key code numbers.
- On 5th September 2018 OURBANK announced it was to create 67 new jobs in the area, and had chosen XXXX city as the location for a new Customer Protection Centre. The purpose of this centre was to be primarily about data- and information-gathering relating to the sources of customers wealth, and thereby to reduce money laundering.

Ironically, just now as I write this I have received a fraud warning text from my bank (see Figure 8, below), which demonstrates an improvement, one year on, in the clarity of their text warnings.

> **OURBANK**
>
> Hi Jonathan. We're aware of fraudulent text messages claiming to come from **OURBANK**. They may even appear in a chain of previous genuine messages from us. If you've any concerns about a message you have received do not reply or call the number provided, instead call us using the number on the back of your bank card or by using the contact details on our website. To unsubscribe from service texts, text **STOPSERV** to....

Figure 8: - OURBANK's improved fraud warning (04/04/19)

To our knowledge, none of our other recommendations to the OURBANK international CEO have, to date, been adopted.

Scam Survivor

Aiming high and maintaining our dignity in our correspondence with this International CEO was another significant factor in our being in the driver's seat of our recovery. Whether or not our correspondence was on the desk of our regional CEO when his local team decided to review our case and restore our funds with compensation, we cannot say.

As pointed out in Step 1 above, there were three further steps that we took after sending this letter to the International CEO. We needed to keep the momentum going, and we didn't wait around for his reply, which was about a month in coming.

- *Contact with our local elected representative.*

- *Contact with the local and or national press.* We decided we didn't want our story in the local press. There was the possibility of an interview on a national radio station. This didn't take place due to the football World Cup affecting their scheduling. This wasn't an interview we sought – it came on the back of our story in the national newspaper.

- *Submission of our formal complaint to the Financial Ombudsman Service (FOS) in London.*

Of course, we knew the police were also looking into our case and both we, and no doubt OURBANK, were placing hope in the small possibility that the fraudsters would be caught and that some, if not all, of our stolen money might be retrieved. This might go some way to explaining the bank's stalling, and our delaying three months before submitting our complaint to the Ombudsman.

It could have been any of the above steps that eventually made the difference. However, it is our firm belief that it was probably the build-up of momentum and the pressure that we brought to bear on OURBANK, and a combination of our overall strategy as outlined above, that led to breakthrough.

In summary, we had started off by drawing up a plan of action and then we worked our plan. I kept a detailed journal, a clear record of everything that happened. We identified who our allies were and built our support team. We established a clear idea of the parameters of our case and what we could reasonably aim for. A professional helped us discern whether we were "grossly negligent", "negligent" or just careless. We communicated well and honourably with OURBANK, maintaining our dignity and self-respect. Finally, we aimed high in terms of who we approached; the statutory organisations, elected representatives, providers of expert advice, OURBANK's own hierarchy, the press and media and, ultimately, the Financial Ombudsman.

◆ Part 3

Know Your Enemy
Know Your Allies

Scammers only succeed because their victims believe them and unwittingly give them access to their accounts or money, or else the victim has not protected their money sufficiently from the cunning and technical know-how of the scammer.

Or both.

In our case it was both. We initially thought that the text from the scammer was really from OURBANK, and we believed what turned out to be a clever deception. This lie was that someone was trying to use our debit card for a large purchase (£2,499) and that we had to act swiftly and give them access to our account so they could stop that purchase going through. Why did we believe them? It was because they knew of a weakness in our smartphones (that we were unaware of), that allowed them to infiltrate our smartphone's SMS function and insert their cunning message into OURBANK's text-stream.

The chink in our armour was our lack of knowledge and awareness about *smishing* and the weakness that exists in every smartphone's set-up. OURBANK hadn't told us us, but neither had we informed ourselves. We were not suspicious enough to question the message that came through, put down the phone and investigate.

Not every victim lacks knowledge about scams. At the outset we heard of the police officers, even fraud experts who had fallen foul of the scammers. However knowledgeable you may be, you can still become a victim of the next new scam or repackaged old one. All it takes is a lapse of vigilance, or ignorance of the latest trick or cunning ploy. However, you can minimise the risk of succumbing by developing a suspicion of every message that comes to you urging you to act quickly in a certain way.

Yes, you could choose to minimise all risk of cyber-crime by never going on the internet and to avoid the purchase of a smartphone. This, of course, would significantly reduce the risk of cyber-crime. Maybe there are some people who can do this without it hugely impacting on their daily life. For those no longer in employment and with a simple lifestyle involving minimal requirement to go online or use cards. For most of us, though, our lives are now dependent on having access to the internet, to emails and to smartphones. Even if you were to cut yourself off from the internet, that wouldn't necessarily keep you from falling victim to ATM or card fraud at the point of sale or from having your card skimmed as you walked down a busy high street or shopping aisle.

Indeed, you might choose to carry out all your purchases using cash withdrawn from a visit to your own bank branch, thereby avoiding having to use ATMs and credit or debit cards in shops. However, increasingly we live in a world of cashless, digital transactions, and it is becoming much harder to operate in the developed world, or even the developing world, without debit or credit cards or an online account. This is reflected in the reduced number of ATMs, the increased number of businesses accepting only card purchases, and the widespread use of contactless payments. All this has been accelerated by the COVID-19 pandemic as people choose to avoid visits to a bricks-and-mortar bank to collect cash, and avoid touching cash that may contribute to the spread of the virus.

So for the vast majority of us, the way forward will be about maintaining and increasing our vigilance with a raised knowledge and an up-to-date awareness of how fraudsters operate. We actively need to take all the practical steps possible to protect ourselves and our devices.

Being forewarned, and well-informed, is to be forearmed. Knowing how our enemy, the fraudster or scammer, operates and evolves is half the battle. We need to also know who is on our side and where to find help and advice.

Everyone with a computer, laptop, or smartphone needs to inform themselves on an ongoing basis and maintain vigilance. We should all make the effort and take the time to keep abreast of the latest scams.

The **Appendices** below give links to some of the most useful web-based advice and information, in particular in the UK and USA – such as some of the statutory support available (i.e. Action Fraud, the FCA, FOS) and the best non-statutory help (i.e. The Consumers' Association *Which?*, *Take Five to Stop Fraud*, and the *Money Saving Expert*). In the USA there is the FBI's "IC3 Centre" (Internet Crime Complaint Centre). In Europe there is Europol, though they point the individual to the anti-fraud service in each member state.

Raising awareness is a key aspect of what these organisations do. One Police force in the UK has developed the *Scamwise Partnership*. Their campaign to raise awareness amongst the general public and thereby reduce fraud, includes the helpful "Scam Test" based on the acronym SCAM:

- **S**-eems too good to be true
- **C**-ontacted out of the blue
- **A**-sked for personal details
- **M**-oney requested

If a cold-caller on your doorstep appears unexpectedly, asks for personal details, and/or requests money – often at the end of a persuasive patter – the best advice is usually to just say "No" politely and firmly, and close the door. Doorstep callers should carry ID, and a phone call to a non-emergency police line (such as 101 in the UK) can usually quickly check the credibility of such a person. As for unsolicited phone-calls, a similarly firm approach is advised, and there are now ways to block unsolicited phone-calls (such as the *Telephone Preference Service TPS*[38] in the UK and the call-barring or call-filtering services that most private telecoms companies offer either freely or at a cheap monthly cost).

If the phone-call is purporting to be from your bank, or about money you supposedly owe a company or the inland-revenue service or whomever, my advice would be to hang up politely, having said you will check in person with your bank or the company concerned. It is important then to make sure that when you lift the phone to call your bank or other company on a trusted number that you either use a different phone, or make sure there is a dialling tone at the other end, signifying that the cold-caller has hung up too. One ploy that scammers have is to stay on the phone at the other end and when you think you have dialled through to your bank you are still talking to the fraudster!

---

38 Telephone Preference Service TPS - The free opt out service enabling one to record one's preference on the official register and not receive unsolicited sales or marketing calls: https://www.tpsonline.org.uk/#. (Accessed 16/2/2020).

Scam Survivor

The *Take Five Campaign* in the UK uses the motto: **STOP, CHALLENGE, PROTECT**. Their advice is sound: "Just because someone knows some personal details – such as your name and address or your mother's maiden name – does not mean they are genuine. They could be a fraudster." Below is their guidance on how to stay safe from financial scams. Remember,

- "Banks or trusted organisations will never contact you asking for your PIN or full password, or to transfer money to a safe account.

- Never give out your personal or financial details unless you are absolutely sure you know who you are dealing with.

- Always question unsolicited approaches asking for information – it could be a scam. Instead contact the company directly using a trusted email or phone number to check the request is genuine.

- Don't be tricked into giving a fraudster access to your details. Never automatically click on a link in an unexpected email or text.

- Remember to always

    - Trust your instincts: If something feels wrong then it is usually right to question it. Fraudsters rely on your defences being down when you're in the comfort of your own home and on people being naturally trusting.

    - Stay in control: Be confident – refuse unusual requests for personal or financial information. It's okay to stop the discussion if you do not feel in control of it.

    - Take Five: Always stop and think before acting. Take Five and say 'My money? My info? I don't think so!'

    - What to watch out for...

    - People aren't always who they say they are.

- Fraudsters use a range of tactics to target people and organisations. - They often impersonate someone else and seek to exploit our naturally trusting natures.
- They may pretend to be from your bank, card-company, police, utility company, a government department or someone else you usually deal with and trust." [39]

It's great advice to take five minutes, even five seconds to pause and think before replying, and a memorable life motto for maintaining vigilance against the scammers is: **STOP, CHALLENGE, PROTECT!**

The Minefield of Scams

There are hundreds of scams doing the rounds. Some will be by telephone, others present on your doorstep or come through the post. These days most occur online or via your phone. Some will combine different technologies. In our case it was a *smishing* scam that involved a three-way combination of text, phone and online.

Action Fraud lists 163 different types of fraud spread across ten categories of fraud:[40]

1. Pensions Fraud

2. Banking and Credit fraud

3. Business Fraud

4. Charity Fraud

5. Financial Investment Fraud

6. Customer Fraud

---

[39] Take Five is a UK-wide national campaign that offers "straight-forward and impartial advice" to help people protect themselves from preventable financial fraud. https://takefive-stopfraud.org.uk/ (accessed 27/5/2020).

[40] Action Fraud list of 163 different types of fraud. https://www.actionfraud.police.uk/a-z-of-fraud (Accessed 15/6/2020).

7. Insurance Fraud
8. Telecoms Fraud
9. Advance Fee Fraud
10. Cyber fraud

So cyber-crime is just one category of fraud among many. However, when you look closer into the different scams in each category, it becomes clear that much of the fraud in the other nine categories will also involve cyber-crime as one element of a combined strategy by fraudsters.

Within just the "cyber fraud" category Action Fraud then lists, in alphabetical order, the following 14 types of online scam:[41]

- Botnet-related fraud
- Click fraud
- Computer hacking
- Computer Software Service frauds
- Domain name scams
- Facility takeover
- Fraud enabling activities
- Internet dialler scam
- Invoice scams
- Malware and computer viruses
- Phishing
- Proxy servers
- Tabnapping
- Website domain name scams

Interestingly, *smishing* does not appear as a heading in this list, though when one goes to the Phishing page, at the bottom of that page is a "See also" section which lists three cyber threats related

[41] Action Fraud list of 14 types of online scam https://www.actionfraud.police.uk/a-z-of-fraud-category/cyber-fraud (Accessed 15/6/2020).

to phishing: *Vishing, Smishing* and *Identity theft and fraud.* The information pages for the first two of these are, sadly, very limited in scope and merely state "*Vishing* is when fraudsters obtain personal details of a victim by phone. Fraudsters can go on to use this personal information to commit fraud".[42] "*Smishing* is when fraudsters obtain personal details of a victim by SMS text messages. Fraudsters can go on to use this personal information to commit fraud".[43] The page on *identity theft and fraud* is much more detailed and helpful.[44]

Below is a short-list and explanations of some of the more common and current cyber-crime threats and how to spot them.[45] This section is included simply to give you a bit more of an idea of how scammers operate. It is by no means an exhaustive list. The **Appendices** section at the end of this book gives a list of reputable organisations that advise on cyber-crime and cyber-security and includes a number of helpful links to online advice and resources.

1. Phishing

Phishers usually try and assume the identity of someone you trust – it could be a friend, a neighbour, a work colleague or your bank – in an attempt to get you to hand over information or click a malicious link on an email, or in a social media platform or a messaging app. such as WhatsApp. The *smishing* scam we fell victim to is just one example of a phishing

---

[42] Action Fraud's page on vishing: https://www.actionfraud.police.uk/a-z-of-fraud/vishing (Accessed 15/6/2020).
[43] Action Fraud's page on smishing: https://www.actionfraud.police.uk/a-z-of-fraud/smishing (Accessed 15/6/2020).
[44] Action Fraud's page on identity fraud and theft: https://www.actionfraud.police.uk/a-z-of-fraud/identity-fraud-and-identity-theft (Accessed 15/6/2020).
[45] Drawn primarily from cyber security company Norton's advice on *The five most popular online scams to be aware of in 2020*: https://uk.norton.com/internetsecurity-online-scams-5-most-popular-scams-in-2020.html (Accessed 22/7/2020).

scam. In our case we were deceived into believing the scammer's text came from OURBANK. The woman "Tanya" skilfully kept up the deception.

The most important step in spotting a phishing attempt is to resist the pressure to act quickly to supposedly protect your money. Taking your time reviewing the email or message will enable you to see possible clues such as poor spelling or grammar in the text. Sometimes a link will not take you where the visible text is indicating. One way to spot this inconsistency on a computer is to hover over a link with your mouse cursor (without clicking) if you're unsure of it. In the bottom left-hand corner, you'll see the full URL – and know if you're being directed to a real or scam website.

2. Fake antivirus software

If you're browsing the web and all of a sudden a pop-up appears saying that your computer is now infected, it is possible that this is an online scam. The aim of fraudulent antivirus software pop-ups and other ads is for you to download free software which may well contain some cyber threat or other such as a virus, malware or ransomware.

It is good advice to ignore flashing pop-up ads or banners that urge you to take action immediately by downloading an application. A reputable antivirus software package will monitor threats in the background and, while it may ask you to take action, it will probably only notify you once the threat has been resolved.

You are also advised to only trust virus information from your own antivirus protection software – and if you don't have one, make sure to install one immediately. Banks may well not reimburse customers who lose money from computers that aren't protected.

3. Easy money scams

These are websites or advertisement which often say you can earn sizeable sums quickly. They then persuade you to hand over personal and financial information. It is a healthy and wise position to assume that schemes promising quick money gained with little effort are not to be trusted. We should all be wary of advertisements that say it takes little or no skill to get involved, that you can determine your own hours or that you need to pay up front to get started.

4. Tech-support scams

Taking the form of either a phone call or an advertisement, tech-support scammers will contact you to tell you that your computer or device is infected – often without even seeing the device beforehand. After prompting the user to download an application that lets them control the computer remotely, the scammers then download actual viruses or try and persuade you that something is wrong with your device. Then they ask for money to fix the problem. It is worth knowing that Google, Microsoft, or Apple and any reliable tech. firm will never call you to tell you that something is wrong with your computer. The most they will do is send an email saying that something is wrong with your device and that you should call them. Before making that call always double check via a Google search that these numbers are the real support numbers.

Similarly, you can avoid being conned by fraudsters, who contact you via email or advertise online to fix or service your device, by getting in touch with the manufacturer of the device itself. Alternatively, finding a reliable computer service and repair business in your local area may well help you avoid the pitfalls of the web.

5. Fake shopping websites

There are numerous fraudulent websites which aim to convince people to part with their money in pursuit of a great discount or deal. E-commerce scam websites tend to create web addresses that are nearly identical to the brand or company name that they are pretending to be. Often there will be a single small spelling difference which the unsuspecting will not see. The victims then end up paying for goods which are either fake or never arrive in the post.

6. Form-jacking

This more recent cyber threat aims at stealing credit card information. This can happen when a genuine e-commerce website is hacked, without the proprietor's knowledge. The fraudsters then redirect you to different URLs in the payment process that look similar to the legitimate website address (with perhaps a single letter added or removed), but actually steal your information. Constant vigilance is the key once you know what scammers can do. The best advice, when making online purchases and before committing to payment, is to double check the URL to make sure you're still on the exact same website that you came from. Checking there is a secure padlock icon to the left or right of the URL in the address window at the top of a website is also a good habit to adopt. All payment pages should also have "https://" at the start of the URL (as opposed to just "http://").[46] If your anti-virus is up-to-date it may also warn you, at the point of a browser search, of a suspicious website or when you go onto an unreliable page.

In the **Appendices** that follow you will find a number of resources that will enable you to discover

---

46 Article: What Is HTTPS, and Why Should I Care? https://www.howtogeek.com/181767/htg-explains-what-is-https-and-why-should-i-care/

more about the different types of fraud, steps to submit claims and where to get professional help. You can learn ways to protect yourself and find the statutory authorities whose job it is to both advise and help victims and inform on protection against fraud. There are links to some press coverage, including our own story, as well as to published research and a helpful literature review for those looking to find out more about fraud typologies and victims.

Appendices

Information and resources for the victim and for those looking to be more vigilant:

    A. Statutory and other bodies dealing with fraud cases (UK)

    B. Statutory and other bodies dealing with fraud cases (USA)

    C. Statutory and other bodies dealing with fraud cases (EU)

    D. Media coverage of fraud cases

    E. Published research on fraud

APPENDIX A:

STATUTORY AND OTHER BODIES DEALING WITH FRAUD CASES (UK)

Appendix A provides a wide range of UK-based organisations that give advice and help regarding fraud for both those wishing to protect themselves, as well as those who have fallen victim to fraud. [In Appendices B and C we also include a list of web-links and organisations in the USA and European Union (EU), whose purpose is to help victims of fraud find the help they need and, if necessary, where to make a claim or file a complaint].

i. Action Fraud - Action Fraud is the UK's national reporting centre for fraud and cyber-crime where you should report fraud if you have been scammed, defrauded or have experienced cyber-crime in England, Wales and Northern Ireland. Action Fraud sits alongside the National Fraud Intelligence Bureau (NFIB) within the City of London Police which is the National policing lead for economic crime:

- URL: https://www.actionfraud.police.uk/what-is-action-fraud

Action Fraud's "A-Z of fraud categories". This is a very useful list of at least 163 different fraud types, giving tips on how to spot or report a scam and how to protect yourself:

- URL: https://www.actionfraud.police.uk/a-z-of-fraud

Action Fraud gives the following guidance on reporting a fraud crime:

- Report it to Action Fraud by calling us on 0300 123 2040 or by using our online reporting tool: https://www.actionfraud.police.uk/reporting
- Report to the FCA – you can report an unauthorised firm or scam to the FCA by contacting their Consumer Helpline on 0800 111 6768 or using our reporting form: https://www.fca.org.uk/consumers/report-scam-us
- You can report nuisance calls and messages to the Information Commissioner's Office using their online reporting tool or by calling 0303 123 1113.

ii. The Financial Ombudsman service (FOS) – This is a service which is free for consumers. People generally contact them about problems with: bank accounts, payments and cards; payment protection insurance (PPI); home, car, travel and other types of insurance; loans and other credit, like car finance; debt collection and repayment problems; mortgages; financial advice, investments and pensions.

- Telephone number: 0800 023 4567
- URL: www.financial-ombudsman.org.uk
- URL: Step-by-step process on how to submit a complaint to the FOS https://www.financial-ombudsman.org.uk/consumers/how-to-complain

- URL: of the Financial Ombudsman's complaints search tool - http://www.ombudsman-decisions.org.uk/
- URL: of the FOS ruling that came closest to our situation: http://www.financial-ombudsman.org.uk/publications/ombudsman-news/116/116-disputed-transactions.html#cs1

iii. **The Financial Conduct Authority (FCA)** – The FCA was established on 1st April 2013, taking over responsibility for conduct and relevant prudential regulation from the Financial Services Authority. Their aim is to ensure that the financial markets are "honest, fair and effective so that consumers get a fair deal". They attempt to do this by regulating the conduct of more than 59,000 businesses. They are the prudential supervisor for 49,000 firms and set specific standards for 19,000 firms.

Financial Conduct Authority information about unauthorised transactions:

- URL: https://www.fca.org.uk/consumers/unauthorised-payments-account
- Report to the FCA – you can report an unauthorised firm or scam to the FCA by contacting their Consumer Helpline on 0800 111 6768 or using our reporting form: https://www.fca.org.uk/consumers/report-scam-us

iv. **Police websites** giving useful advice, information and help on fraud:

The **Metropolitan Police**'s 2020 edition of their publication *"The Little Book of Fraud Scams"* (5th edition):

- URL: https://www.met.police.uk/ SysSiteAssets/media/downloads/central/ advice/fraud/met/the-little-book-of- big-scams.pdf

This is the **City of London Police**'s useful website giving contacts for advice about fraud and cyber-crime:

- URL: https://www.cityoflondon.police. uk/advice/advice-and-information/ fa2/fraud/useful-contacts-for-fraud- cybercrime-advice/

This is the **Police Service of Northern Ireland**'s (PSNI) valuable website aimed at educating the public on scams of different kinds through the *SCAMWISE* campaign:

- URL: https://www.psni.police.uk/crime/ fraud/scamwise-ni/
- URL: https://www.psni.police.uk/ globalassets/crime/fraud/scamwise/ final-psni_lbobs_fourth-edition_ online.pdf

v. **Financial Fraud Action** (**FFA**) – the FFA is a government initiative promoting the "Take Five to Stop Fraud" campaign. It is a national fraud awareness campaign launched to help customers "take back control and beat financial fraud – particularly the growing problem of bank transfer scams".

- URL: https://www.financialfraudaction.org. uk/wp-content/uploads/2016/07/Take-Five- customer-advice-guide-081117.pdf

vi. **Take Five to Stop Fraud** – Take Five is a UK-wide national campaign that offers "straight-forward and impartial advice" to help people protect themselves from preventable financial fraud. This includes email deception and phone-based scams as well as online fraud – particularly where criminals impersonate trusted organisations.

- URL: https://takefive-stopfraud.org.uk/

vii. **Which? The Consumers' Association** – describe themselves as "championing the cause for consumers since 1957". They are a charity that campaigns on behalf of the consumer, and also provides free advice to the public on a wide range of matters such as scams and dangerous goods.

Which? The Charity – the Consumers' Association is a registered charity (Charity No 296072) and sits at the top of the Which? Group. The Consumers' Association is responsible for all Which? campaigns and the development of Which? policy. The majority of the research included in the various Which? publications is also undertaken by the Consumers' Association.

Which? Products and Services – all the commercial operations are carried on through *Which? Limited* (Company No 677665) and its subsidiary companies. These activities include various magazines and books, digital products, *Which? Legal, Which? Money Helpline, Which? Switch, Which? Trusted Traders, Which? Wills* and *Which? Money Compare*.

- URL: https://www.which.co.uk/about-which/who-we-are
- URL: https://campaigns.which.co.uk/scams-fraud-safeguard/
- URL: https://whichcouk.bsd.net/page/s/which-scam-alerts (a free service of emailed alerts with information on the latest scams)
- URL: https://www.which.co.uk/consumer-rights/l/types-of-scams
- URL: https://www.which.co.uk/later-life-care/home-care/scams-and-older-people/common-online-scams-apwby4t6gp61

(more information on common online scams, how to protect yourself and get help if you're scammed)

- URL: https://www.which.co.uk/later-life-care/home-care/scams-and-older-people/understanding-online-scams-a51813g859kw (more information on the latest scams, how to protect yourself and get help if you're scammed)
- URL: https://www.which.co.uk/news/2020/03/confirmation-of-payee-which-banks-are-ready-to-offer-vital-name-checking-service/ this page gives information on the new "Confirmation of Payee" (CoP) service to prevent APP fraud, and says which UK banks are ready to offer a vital name-checking service.
- [*Confirmation of Payment (COP)* – For information on how CoP works and which UK banks have signed up to this service see: https://www.which.co.uk/news/2020/03/confirmation-of-payee-which-banks-are-ready-to-offer-vital-name-checking-service/]
- URL: https://conversation.which.co.uk/money/scam-text-message-from-bank/#more-102655

viii. Money Saving Expert

This is the website of Martin Lewis, the well-known UK expert on money matters. His fraud page lists articles by his organisation on the latest big scams and how to spot and avoid them:

- URL: https://www.moneysavingexpert.com/news/tag/fraud/
- URL: Money Saving Expert's list of "Best free antivirus software": https://www.moneysavingexpert.com/broadband-and-tv/free-anti-virus-software/

The above website also points out that "If you're not protected and someone gets hold of your passwords, or accesses your bank account or other financial products, you may find it harder to get your money back. The burden of proof is on the bank to show you didn't act with due care, but it is best to be safe.

For more on what to do if you think you've been defrauded, read the ID (Identity) Fraud Protection guide":

- URL: https://www.moneysavingexpert.com/credit-cards/identity-fraud/

ix. Anti-virus and cyber-security companies

Norton, one of the leading cyber-security and anti-virus software companies, has its own list of common scams, which are all website-based. There are many other cyber-security and anti-virus software companies offering useful advice and protection. Norton is just listed by way of example. Some good antivirus software is free.[47] Everyone with a computer, PC, laptop, or phone that has access to the internet should ensure they have appropriate and up-to-date anti-virus software installed. Hackers are able also to access wi-fi routers, and infiltrate any number of household devices that may be connected to the internet, from smart televisions to baby monitors that can be viewed remotely. Readers are advised to investigate the cyber-security of any connected appliances they have and ensure they have appropriate protection in place.

---

[47] Money Saving Expert's list of "Best free antivirus software": https://www.moneysavingexpert.com/broadband-and-tv/free-anti-virus-software/ (Accessed 22/6/2020).

Norton's advice on How to Avoid Online Scams

- URL: https://uk.norton.com/internetsecurity-online-scams.html?inid=nortoncom_nav_internetsecurity-online-scams_homepage:home

Norton's advice on *The five most popular online scams to be aware of in 2020*

- URL: https://uk.norton.com/internetsecurity-online-scams-5-most-popular-scams-in-2020.html

Norton's advice on How to protect against phishing scams

- URL: https://uk.norton.com/internetsecurity-online-scams-how-to-protect-against-phishing-scams.html

Norton's advice on Coronavirus phishing emails: How to protect against COVID-19 scams

- URL: https://uk.norton.com/internetsecurity-online-scams-coronavirus-phishing-scams.html

APPENDIX B:

STATUTORY AND OTHER BODIES DEALING WITH FRAUD CASES (USA)

Appendix B provides information and contact details for US victims of cyber-crime. In the USA the Federal Trade Commission provides data and advice on fraud and fraud prevention. There is the FBI's "IC3 Centre" (Internet Crime Complaint Centre).[48] Their web-portal lists fraud alerts for consumers and industry, provides "Internet crime prevention tips", a catalogue of "Internet crime schemes", as well as an area where individuals or firms can "File a Complaint". The "Stay Safe Online" resource (part of the National Cyber Security Alliance) provides helpful signposting advice with a useful list of organisations and addresses for those falling victim to various kinds of cyber-crime in the USA. These include online identity theft, financial fraud, stalking, bullying, hacking, e-mail spoofing, information piracy and forgery, intellectual property crime, malware attacks and Social Security fraud.[49]

---

48 The FBI's "IC3 Centre" (Internet Crime Complaint Centre) lists fraud alerts for consumers and industry, provides "Internet crime prevention tips", a catalogue of "Internet crime schemes", as well as a page where individuals or firms can "File a Complaint": https://www.ic3.gov/default.aspx (Accessed 05/05/2020).
49 STAY SAFE ONLINE (part of the National Cyber Security Alliance)

i. The Federal Trade Commission:

The FTC website gives a helpful list entitled Ten Things You Can Do to Avoid Fraud. This document is available as a free downloadable PDF and is available in seven languages in addition to English.

- URL: https://www.consumer.ftc.gov/articles/0060-10-things-you-can-do-avoid-fraud

ii. The FBI's "IC3 Centre" (Internet Crime Complaint Centre):

- URL: https://www.ic3.gov/default.aspx

This web-portal lists fraud alerts for consumers and industry, provides "Internet crime prevention tips", a catalogue of "Internet crime schemes", as well as an area where individuals or firms can "File a Complaint". Their list and descriptions of different types of fraud includes the following:

- Auction Fraud
- Counterfeit Cashier's Check
- Credit Card Fraud
- Parcel Courier Email Scheme
- Escrow Services Fraud
- Identity Theft
- Internet Extortion
- Investment Fraud
- Nigerian Letter or "419"
- Phishing/Spoofing
- Ponzi/Pyramid
- Reshipping
- Spam
- Third Party Receiver of Funds

---

offers a very useful, informative and practical web-resource which includes this two-page pdf file https://staysafeonline.org/wp-content/uploads/2017/09/What-To-Do-If-You-Are-a-Victim-of-Cybercrime.pdf (Accessed 05/05/2020).

iii. STAY SAFE ONLINE (part of the National Cyber Security Alliance):

- URL: https://staysafeonline.org

This is a very useful, informative and practical web-resource which includes this two-page pdf file:

- URL: https://staysafeonline.org/wp-content/uploads/2017/09/What-To-Do-If-You-Are-a-Victim-of-Cybercrime.pdf

This PDF is a gold-mine of useful information and web addresses to help victims of all kinds of online crime and fraud. It answers questions such as: Should I report cyber-crime? Who should I contact? It includes tips such as Collect and Keep Evidence, and for different types of cyber-crime such as online identity theft, financial fraud, stalking, bullying, hacking, e-mail spoofing, information piracy and forgery. In addition, it deals with intellectual property crime, malware attacks, and Social Security fraud. It gives helpful advice on whom to contact depending on the crime: Local law enforcement, IC3, the Federal Trade Commission, or Your Local Victim Service Provider. Its list of other useful organisations to contact in different situations includes the following:

- Anti-Phishing Working Group (reportphishing@antiphishing.org)

- Better Business Bureau (investigates disagreements between businesses and customers; www.bbb.org/consumer-complaints/file-a-complaint/get-started)

- CyberTipLine, operated by the National Center for Missing & Exploited Children (investigates cases of online sexual exploitation of children; 1-800-843-5678 or www.cybertipline.com)

- Electronic Crimes Task Forces and Working Groups (https://legacy.secretservice.gov/ectf.shtml)

- The Secret Service (investigates fraudulent use of currency; www.secretservice.gov/field_offices.shtml)
- StopFraud.Gov Victims of Fraud Resources (www.stopfraud.gov/victims.html)
- U.S. Computer Emergency Readiness Team (www.us-cert.gov) · U.S.Department of Justice (www.justice.gov/criminal/cybercrime)
- U.S. Postal Inspection Service (investigates fraudulent online auctions and other cases involving the mail; https://www.uspis.gov/report/)
- Your State Attorney General (the National Association of Attorneys General keeps a current contact list at URL: www.naag.org/current-attorneys-general.php)

Appendix C:

Statutory and Other Bodies Dealing with Fraud Cases (EU)

Appendix C provides some information and contact details for anyone falling victim to cyber-crime in the EU. In the European Union the EU-wide police force "Europol" has an online webpage of limited value, where victims of cyber-crime can get some help on reporting an attack.[50]

Their "Report Cyber-crime Online" portal:

- URL: https://www.europol.europa.eu/report-a-crime/report-cybercrime-online
- This directs anyone who has fallen victim to cyber-crime to the reporting website of their own country. It states: "Reporting mechanisms in the EU will vary from one country to another. In Member States which do not have a dedicated online option in place, individuals are advised to go to their local police station to lodge a complaint". The UK link on this page, for example, directs you to the UK's "Action Fraud" website. The German link takes you to the home page of the German police – so obviously more digging would be

---

50 Europol's "Report Cyber-crime Online" portal directs anyone who has fallen victim to cyber-crime to the reporting website of their own country https://www.europol.europa.eu/report-a-crime/report-cybercrime-online. (Accessed 05/05/2020).

needed to get you to the specific help available for victims of fraud. The French link on the Europol page does a little better in that it directs one to a page where the individual may report "illicit internet content" – so not specific necessarily to cyber-crime.

❖ Appendix D:

Media Coverage of Fraud Cases

The **i-newspaper** full article covering our story (4-6-2018):

- URL: https://inews.co.uk/inews-lifestyle/money/warning-over-sophisticated-bank-text-scam-that-conned-a-university-lecturer-out-of-25000-159932

The Times ACTION FRAUD INVESTIGATION - *Action Fraud staff sneer at "moron" victims and nap on the job:*

- URL: https://www.thetimes.co.uk/article/action-fraud-staff-sneer-at-moron-victims-and-nap-on-the-job-28mm27pps

Appendix E:

Published Research on Fraud (UK)

University of Portsmouth's report and literature review on Fraud typologies and victims (2009), produced with the National Fraud Authority and endorsed by ACPO (Association of Chief Police Officers), and the Office of Fair Trading. While this is already dated, it includes much that has lasted the test of time. Especially useful are the sections on the perpetrators of frauds, on the techniques of fraudsters (such as having a professional and legitimate appearance, a good sales pitch, selling a dream, and a "legal hinterland"), on the characteristics of victims of fraud, on victim typologies, on the profile of victims (i.e. the typical age and gender depending on the type of scam) and on the impact upon the victim:

- URL: https://researchportal.port.ac.uk/portal/files/1926122/NFA_report3_16.12.09.pdf

Acknowledgements

The journey of recovery from the scam to getting this book to publication could not have been completed without the support, patience, encouragement and wisdom of my dear wife, Tricia. I am also grateful to those various "allies" mentioned in the book without whose contributions, wisdom and advice I wouldn't have known what to do, the order in which to do it, or gained the courage to pick myself up and keep going to point of resolution.

So thank you, in particular to our retired lawyer friend "P." who gave us the invaluable early guidance in terms of steps to take and the dogged and enlightening *Which?* adviser "M." whose research uncovered key archive rulings giving us the courage to believe in our case. My thanks also to our engaged, supportive and steadfast Member of Parliament "Mr. A." who gave advice and sacrificed his time from his busy schedule. His trenchant letters written and meetings arranged with key people made such a difference to our morale. We believe these had a significant impact on the final outcome of our campaign. You were all so valuable in different ways and at different points in the process.

Thanks also to the fantastic team at the Self-Publishing School whose enthusiasm, knowledge and motivational abilities helped me bring this book to publication. I am also very grateful to my editor Joel, my cover designer Jenny, my proof-reader, those who read my draft in advance and fed back valuable thoughts and suggestions, and those who kindly wrote endorsements.

Finally, thanks to our wider circle of family and friends, whose love, concern, and timely interventions gave us the strength and support to persevere and keep going all the way.

ABOUT THE AUTHOR

Jonathan Leakey (PGCE, PhD) lives in Northern Ireland with his wife Patricia, who is from County Antrim. They have two adult children. Jonathan grew up in East Africa and came to the UK at the age of ten. His teaching career as a French and German specialist spanned 34 years, progressing through three different sectors of education: 14 years in secondary schools on Merseyside, England, three years in the Northern Ireland Hotel and Catering College and 17 at Ulster University. His doctorate and subsequent research was in effectiveness research in computer-assisted language learning (CALL). He has authored a number of articles in his specialist field and written a book "*Evaluating Computer-Assisted Language Learning*". Since retiring from teaching, he has been doing freelance translation as well as cross-community reconciliation work. In his free time he enjoys hill-walking, gardening, writing, drawing and painting.

Printed in Great Britain
by Amazon